Praise for

LESSONS *from the* ADMIRAL

"Born to lead, Navy Captain Mark Fava learned leadership as a twenty-seven-year-old admiral's aide, the 'best of the best.' A superb officer and a true gentleman, Mark was the loop who wore the gold-and-blue braided aiguillette, whose job was to know his boss's every thought and word, and to anticipate his every decision and move. Now, in his first book, he passes on the wisdom of the leaders who taught him how to lead over his thirty years in the Navy Reserve, law practice, and business. Commit the leadership wisdom in this book to memory. Practice it every day as you rise in the ranks, and someday, you, too, will lead others, whatever your walk of life."

J. MICHAEL LUTTIG, former US Court of Appeals judge

"From commanding a Navy P-3 squadron to the corporate C-suite, Mark Fava has lived and breathed leadership. Whether you are a leader or a follower aspiring to be a leader, this book is for you! An inspiring and entertaining story based on the bond of trust between an admiral and his aide, Fava's *Lessons from the Admiral* provides powerful insight. Read this book, and you will lead better!"

LUKE M. MCCOLLUM, Vice Admiral (ret.), US Navy, 14th Chief of Navy Reserve

"An insightful and enjoyable read with artful storytelling. At numerous points in the book, I found myself thinking, *Man, I wish I had known that sooner*. Practice these lessons, and your path to success will be much smoother."

GREG RIGGS, Executive Coach and former Senior Vice President, General Counsel, and Chief Corporate Affairs Officer, Delta Air Lines

"In *Lessons from the Admiral*, Mark Fava gives us timeless lessons that are as applicable to a new employee or middle manager as they are to a senior executive: know your boss, listen to all stakeholders, be prepared, and serve with a purpose."

HANK MOLINENGO, Rear Admiral, JAGC, USN (Ret.) and former Senior Associate Dean for Administrative Affairs, The George Washington University Law School

"You don't have to be a lawyer, aviator, or veteran to enjoy this book. A masterful and entertaining storyteller, Mark Fava gives us ageless wisdom and a road map to success in *Lessons from the Admiral*. A must-read for current leaders and aspiring leaders alike."

JOSH LINKNER, five-time tech entrepreneur, *New York Times* bestselling author, and venture capitalist

"In *Lessons from the Admiral*, Mark Fava reflects on his real-life learnings while serving in a demanding and high-pressure position, yielding practical lessons that paved the way for him to become a successful military officer and high-level attorney. It's an entertaining read, chock-full of great leadership advice."

HONORABLE ROBERT L. SUMWALT, Chairman, National Transportation Safety Board (2017-2021)

www.amplifypublishinggroup.com

Lessons from the Admiral: Naval Wisdom and Sea Stories for Leaders

Second printing. This Amplify Publishing edition printed in 2025.

For more information, please contact:
Amplify Publishing, an imprint of Amplify Publishing Group
620 Herndon Parkway, Suite 220
Herndon, VA 20170
info@amplifypublishing.com

Library of Congress Control Number: 2024907318

CPSIA Code: PRV0225B

ISBN-13: 979-8-89138-217-6

Printed in the United States

Mom was my first teacher. She was a fierce defender of our family of five. At the age of eighty-two, she was diagnosed with amyotrophic lateral sclerosis, or ALS. It is an incredibly cruel disease that slowly takes your body, but not your mind. Never once did she complain.

I read this book out loud to her in its final stages. She gave me a thumbs-up. "Good book," she tried to say. I love her and miss her.

Dad never left her side during that time.

My first book is dedicated to Mom and Dad.

LESSONS *from the* ADMIRAL

NAVAL WISDOM *and* SEA STORIES *for* LEADERS

MARK C. FAVA

CONTENTS

INTRODUCTION

I have gotten every job I ever wanted. I studied and worked hard, but I started early in my career by closely observing the leaders I worked for, especially my bosses. You should too, and I'll tell you why.

This book is about what I learned serving one of those leaders, a navy admiral. I was the Admiral's aide more than thirty years ago as a young naval officer. What I learned from that job will help you succeed just as it has done for me.

The Admiral was a senior naval aviator and a great boss. He was a fatherly figure. I was his third aide, so he knew what to expect from the role. He was a salty admiral who had "fired" his first aide. A P-3 Orion pilot, he had gotten his start flying the predecessor to the P-3, a navy seaplane called the P5M Marlin. He had also commanded a group of navy minesweepers.

When I had been in my new job as his aide for two weeks, he called me into his office, shut the door, and said, "Take a seat, Lieutenant."

I sat in one of the high-backed, black leather chairs in front of his desk. After some small talk, the Admiral's tone changed.

"Let's discuss this job and my expectations," he said. "You are going to do a lot of things and see a lot of things as my aide. Many are going to be great, and some are going to be . . . well . . . not so great. Many tasks will be well above your pay grade, and others will be well below your pay grade. I need you to perform exceptionally well whether you're completing a great task or a not-so-great task. You understand that, Lieutenant?"

"Yes, sir, I understand."

As I look back, that was part of what I now call the "initial guidance." At the time, I had no idea what I would see or do, but I knew that the correct answer was an affirmative one.

I would learn so much more over the next seventeen months.

I wrote this book for anyone who has ever worn a military uniform and enjoys a good sea story and especially for anyone who wants to grow in their career—military or civilian. I wrote this book to pass on the experiences and knowledge I gained from that job as an admiral's aide.

This book is for middle managers who want to be executives, associate lawyers who want to become partners, and junior military officers who aspire to be commanding officers. All are in the same stage of their lives. The only difference is what they wear to work. If this describes where you are in your career, I wrote this book for you.

You are in the prime of your life. You want to take care of your family and send your children to the best schools. You work hard to save for their college and your retirement. You want to keep your partner happy, buy a house, and have enough money to travel and enjoy good vacations. You want to be promoted to roles of greater responsibility. You want to have leverage and the ability to change jobs. You want to be a leader.

This book offers lessons that will help you achieve all that. I'll pass along to you the habits and traits that have led to my success for over thirty years. These are lessons from what I saw, did, and learned as an admiral's aide.

Putting the knowledge you gain from this book into practice will make you stand out among your peers as a high performer. You will be organized. You will gain an understanding of how executives think and what they appreciate. You will enjoy your job because you'll be achieving success in your daily routine. Those evaluating you will identify you as a future leader. And you will be promoted!

The lessons I learned from the Admiral I still practice today as a senior executive at a Fortune 100 company. I have used these skills to excel in my careers as a lawyer and naval officer. I served in the navy for thirty years as a naval flight officer. I've also enjoyed a successful career as a lawyer, and I managed both careers at the same time. The knowledge I gained as an officer in the navy, I applied as a civilian lawyer. What I learned as a civilian lawyer, I used in the navy.

In the navy, I was steadily promoted to higher ranks and greater roles of responsibility. After six years on active duty as a naval flight officer, I went to law school and transferred to the Navy Reserve. I served another twenty-four years, ultimately retiring from the navy as a captain. I was the commanding officer of three units, including an aviation squadron.

While I was advancing in the military, I pursued my passion for law and became a successful aviation lawyer. I have been a federal judicial law clerk, working for a federal judge; a litigation associate; and a partner at a major law firm. I built a national aviation law practice at that firm, and I have also been an executive in-house lawyer for two major corporations. The first was Delta Air Lines, where I was the chief operations attorney on 9/11. I now work for the world's largest aircraft manufacturer, the Boeing Company, where I have been for over fourteen years.

Throughout my career, in addition to getting every job I've ever wanted, I have also received the promotions I thought I deserved. I rose to the rank of captain in the Navy Reserve and a vice president at Boeing. Now I mentor others about what I learned and what senior leaders like me look for when identifying people like you as future leaders deserving of promotions and roles of greater responsibility.

The skills necessary for success as both a lawyer and a naval officer are the same. These skills—such as attention to detail, knowing what is important to your boss, punctuality, dependability, credibility, and integrity—are transferable to any career, and applying them consistently has resulted in my lifelong success. In fact, these skills are the same ones that will lead to advancement in a leadership role in most professions.

I have always been an "active learner," observing the leaders around me, which have included admirals, judges, general counsel lawyers, senior operational vice presidents, CEOs, and members of corporate boards of directors. The lessons I've gained have become the woven fabric of my leadership habits. Much of how I lead comes from practices that I picked up from others. From the good leaders—like the Admiral—I have emulated their behavior and incorporated their practices. From the bad leaders, I learned just as much—about what not to do, how I don't want to act, and who I will not become!

Those senior to you are evaluating you every day. Your leaders are developing their succession plans. You want to be a part of those plans. So let's get started. It's time to stand out like a leader and be successful in your job.

You need to know what I learned from the Admiral. So let's go back to his office, where it all began.

Chapter 1

KNOW WHAT IS IMPORTANT TO YOUR BOSS

I learned a lot as a twenty-seven-year-old admiral's aide in the navy. I especially learned about leadership, servitude, accountability, integrity, and responsibility.

As I sat in front of his desk during my first few weeks as his aide, the Admiral laid out his expectations for me. As I mentioned earlier, his first requirement was that I perform exceptionally well at *all* assigned tasks.

His initial guidance continued:

Be on time.

"I like to be on time. So let's never be late. You understand that?"

"Yes, sir," I responded.

Confidentiality matters.

"In this job as the loop, you are an extension of my eyes and ears," he said. "You are with me wherever I go. You see and hear what I see and hear, and you remember it. Whatever you see and hear is my business, the business of a navy admiral, and no one else's business. You got that?"

"Yes, sir," I said.

Tell me what I need to hear.

"I will trust your judgment and rely on you to tell me the truth," he stated. "Almost everyone else will agree with me because I am the admiral. When we are behind closed doors, you can 'request permission to speak freely,' and then we take off the stars and bars and speak to each other man-to-man. I will rely on you to keep me out of trouble. Don't let me do anything stupid. Got it?" he asked.

"Yes, sir."

He wore silver stars on the collar of his uniform. I wore silver lieutenant bars, or "railroad tracks," as we called them.

Unconditional allegiance.

"We can disagree and debate behind closed doors, but once I make a decision, the discussion is over. You support and execute that decision. Got it?" he stated.

"Yes, sir."

The stars belong to the admiral.

"Now, these stars are mine," he said, pointing to the silver stars on his collar. "You can use them, but use them sparingly—if and only when you have to. You understand that, Loop?"

"Yes, sir, I understand," I said.

"Good," he said. "Do these things, and we will get along just fine."

This conversation lasted less than ten minutes. It was the most important conversation of my seventeen months as an admiral's aide and one of the most important in my life as a naval flight officer, a lawyer, and a leader.

GETTING TO THE ADMIRAL

The job as an admiral's aide was my second tour of duty in the navy. The day after I graduated from the University of North Carolina at Chapel Hill in 1985, my father, a navy captain at the time, commissioned me into the navy. I went to flight school in Pensacola, Florida, to become a naval flight officer, or NFO. Pensacola is the "Cradle of Naval Aviation" because all naval aviators start there.

In Pensacola, I struggled through a rigorous academic and physical training program. It included courses in aerodynamics, meteorology, aircraft navigation and communication, and aircraft emergency procedures.

When not in the classroom, I was running; boxing; swimming a mile in full flight gear in a hot, chlorinated indoor pool; getting dunked in an aircraft and helicopter dunker; or learning land survival techniques. I ingested a lot of chlorinated water in the pools and chewed on pine needles during my week in the woods for land survival training.

Back then, my only goal was to qualify as a naval flight officer and get the coveted Wings of Gold. Nothing else mattered—except an occasional cold beer.

Friday afternoons found us at the Officers' Club or in downtown Pensacola at Trader Jon's. Thousands of student naval aviators had hung out at Traders over the years, covering the walls in dollar bills, squadron patches and stickers, and leather name tags. I spent most of each weekend studying. I went to church on Sunday, praying that I would make it through the program.

Two years later, I received my NFO wings. My mom and dad pinned them on me. I then got three-year orders to my first choice for a duty station: Naval Air Station, Jacksonville, Florida. The navy assigned me to the VP-56 Dragons, a land-based P-3 Orion squadron. The P-3 is a large, four-engine propeller aircraft. We specialized in maritime surveillance and antisubmarine warfare.

From 1987 to 1990, I flew thousands of miles all around the world chasing Soviet submarines in the P-3. It was the height of the Cold War. Our aircrew consisted of three pilots, two NFOs like me, and seven enlisted aircrew specialists.

In early 1990, when I finished my initial "sea tour" in Jacksonville, Florida, I was considering a job as a naval flight officer instructor that would allow me to stay in Jacksonville. A mentor JAG lawyer approached me about applying for a job that many considered to be a prestigious position for a high-performing junior officer, an admiral's aide.

On his advice, I applied for the position of aide to the top East Coast admiral in my naval aviation community. He was located in Brunswick, Maine—the other East Coast P-3 base.

My application package included all my military performance reports, called Fitness Reports; the awards I'd received from the navy; and an endorsement letter from my commanding officer. A few weeks later, the aide-selection person from the Pentagon notified me that the Admiral would be interviewing me as one of three final candidates. I completed a cordial yet intensive interview with the Admiral a few weeks after that.

Not long thereafter, the selection office informed me that I had gotten the job. The Admiral was going to call me to tell me so. It was not an offer, because once in the selection process, I had committed to taking the job if the Admiral selected me. I would be getting two-year orders soon to leave sunny Jacksonville for the much colder duty station in Brunswick, Maine.

I left my first squadron tour a "superstar" according to my detaching fitness report. My commanding officer wrote:

> "LT Fava is a superstar! He has set the standard for excellence among the junior officers within my squadron through consistently outstanding performance and is

> accordingly ranked 1 of 37 exceptionally talented lieutenants. He was recognized by the Association of Naval Aviation as 'VP NFO of the year for 1989.' Additionally, he was personally selected as the flag aide for commander patrol wings, Atlantic. He has earned my strongest possible recommendation for accelerated promotion, VP department head selection, and eventual aviation command."

Back then, language in fitness reports was "over the top." Regardless, that fitness report was flattering, and I was anxious and excited about what was ahead.

My trip to Maine was uneventful. I drove up Interstate 95 to Brunswick, taking just one day off on the way, as the current aide was ready to leave. I had to "hit the deck running," as we say in the navy.

The hardest part of the move was leaving a strikingly beautiful young lady whom I'd met just a few months before in Jacksonville. I knew I could not take her with me, as I was going to need to focus all my time and energy on the Admiral.

So I kissed her goodbye and left her in Jacksonville. Six years later, she would become my wife.

A FLAG AIDE

The US Navy website states: "Ever wondered what an Admiral does for a living? Want to learn an organization from the TOP DOWN? Flag aide jobs are a fantastic way to gain experience and insight on how the navy operates. As an aide, you get to handle many of the Admiral's personal and administrative matters. It is a challenging but highly rewarding duty for Junior Officers with strong demonstrated performance . . ."

THE AIGUILLETTE

The aide is known in the navy as "the loop" because of the aiguillette that aides wear as part of their uniform. An aiguillette is a gold-and-blue braided loop that attaches to the top of the left shoulder of an officer who works for an admiral. Aides for one-star and two-star rear admirals wear an aiguillette with two loops. Aides who work for three-star or vice admirals wear a thicker, three-loop aiguillette. The aiguillettes for aides for the chief of naval operations and the president, as the commander in chief, have many more braids. The more loops, the bigger the boss.

So there I was in the Admiral's office. A superstar with two-year orders and a new boss. Little did I know it, but I had a *lot* to learn!

WHAT I LEARNED

Here are the first things I knew. I knew within the first few weeks of my job as an aide what was important to the Admiral. He was clear in his expectations.

Over my career, I have found that bosses measure your performance by whether you meet their expectations. In the years since that discussion with the Admiral, I have always found it important for a boss to tell me what their expectations are. If they don't tell me, I find the appropriate time early in the job to ask.

You have to know the measuring stick to be successful. I quickly learned that my success depended on following my boss's guidance and meeting his expectations.

That concept is true in any job. Whether you like it or not, your success depends on meeting your boss's expectations. That's a simple proposition.

From day one, it is important to know what is important to your boss with respect to the role they want you to perform. Do you know what your boss expects of you? You need to know sooner rather than later if you want to get promoted.

Chapter 2

KNOW YOUR BOSS

As an admiral's aide, I needed to know my boss better than anyone else. Some say an aide gets to know their boss as well as, if not better than, the boss's spouse.

I was with the Admiral from when he woke up in the morning, usually well before sunrise, until he went to sleep. This included many weekends and holidays. I woke up before him and went to sleep long after he did. I used that quiet time for planning, schedule review, engagement confirmation, and event preparation. Double-checking every detail of the day's schedule was the only way to succeed and survive as an aide.

WHAT I KNEW

I handled a lot of sensitive matters—both personal and administrative.

I knew the Admiral's shirt and pants sizes and what he liked to eat and drink. I knew the time he went to bed at night and the time he woke up.

I knew whom he liked, and more importantly, whom he back-slapped and glad-handed but really did *not* like.

I knew his wife's and children's names and birthdays. I also knew his wedding anniversary and his dog's name. I knew the prescription medications he took.

WHAT I DID

I wrote his speeches and drafted his official correspondence. I attended most of his meetings. I took mental and written notes of what he heard and said.

I noted the commitments he made.

I planned his daily schedule down to the minute. I managed his calendar and all his travel. I traveled with him around the world.

I ate dinner with his family and went on work and family vacations with him. I picked up his dry cleaning and drove his car.

My desk in the headquarters building was the first one outside the Admiral's office door. I screened all his incoming calls, and I initiated all his outgoing calls.

No one got to see or speak to the Admiral without going through me. I was the gatekeeper.

Wherever we went, I carried a special "admiral's survival and repair kit" in my briefcase. It included his favorite black pens, red felt-tip pens for document editing (the color red is reserved for the admiral or commanding officer of a navy unit), three-by-five white index cards, an extra set of his military insignia—including gold pilot wings—his rank stars, and his rack of ribbons. I had breath mints, aspirin, Afrin, Visine, a small sewing kit, a shoeshine kit, and his prescription glasses.

WHAT I SAW

I saw him getting dressed in the morning and wearing only boxer shorts, white T-shirts, and black socks. I told him when I noticed he had left his zipper open after a head call. I assisted him if he cut himself shaving or had bloodshot eyes.

I inspected his uniform before he left his room or the office. I made sure he'd pinned on his gold aviator wings, military ribbons, and uniform insignia perfectly per the navy's uniform regulations: ribbons straight and parallel to the deck, name tag properly positioned a quarter inch above the pocket, and his "gig line"—or belt line—perfectly aligned with his zipper. I ensured no loose threads or "Irish pennants" hung from his uniform, no lint was on his black winter uniform, and no scuff marks were on his summer white shoes.

I saw him arguing with his wife.

I accidentally walked in on him when he was on the toilet. I briefed him as we stood side by side at the urinals.

I knew the Admiral so well that I could anticipate what he would do and say.

THE HEAD

During the two-week turnover with my predecessor, Lieutenant Samuel Jackson, he told me: "Wherever you go with the Admiral, always know where the nearest head is on your route of travel and at your destination."

I always had to know exactly where I was going before I got there and where to find the restrooms once I got there.

The first couple of times I got out of the official navy vehicle with the Admiral, as we walked into the building for a meeting, he would say, "I'm going to duck into the head quickly and be right back. You see, Loop, at my age, you never pass up an opportunity to go to the head."

Got it, I thought.

Soon I was leading him to the nearest men's head without a word spoken. I knew the routine. He knew that I knew the routine.

Good aides anticipate the admiral's every move, action, and ultimate decision. Equally important, a good aide ensures there is no visible confusion along the way. An admiral has to look like an admiral, not like a confused and lost jackass.

"You never keep the Admiral waiting, and you never, ever, want to embarrass the Admiral," my predecessor, Sam, told me.

WOODEN TOOTHPICKS

In addition to knowing the location of the men's head, Sam briefed me that when the Admiral finished a meal, he would sometimes ask for a wooden toothpick.

Before Sam was commissioned as a naval officer, he was an enlisted sergeant in the prestigious 101st Airborne Division of the army. He still spoke very directly, like a sergeant. He was pretty stiff and didn't have much of a sense of humor.

During my turnover with him, Sam opened his small handheld portfolio (which we affectionately called our "brain") and stated, "Now the Admiral, he likes wooden toothpicks. So I guess I won't be needing these anymore."

He pulled three wooden toothpicks, individually wrapped in clear plastic, out of his brain and handed them to me. "Make sure you always have these with you," he said.

What the hell have I gotten myself into? I thought.

Back then, much of the camaraderie in the navy was generated by pranks. I wondered if this was a joke my predecessor was playing on me.

Without hesitation, I put the toothpicks into my new handheld portfolio "brain" and forgot about them.

THE ADMIRAL'S PILLOW

About a month into the job, we went on our first trip out of the country to visit one of the P-3 squadrons under the Admiral's command. They were operating out of Thule, Greenland. We flew up in a P-3 from Brunswick with other senior officers on the Admiral's staff. We had just departed Canadian airspace, heading over the Atlantic Ocean, when Commander Timmy McNamara, the wing operations officer, came over to me.

The Admiral had slipped into the cockpit to get some "stick time" and fly for a while. Pilots love to fly, no matter their age, and he was no exception. Doing so allowed him to shoot the shit with the squadron's pilots. Even better, it allowed me to relax after what had been a hectic and dark early-morning departure.

I was in the aft of the P-3, where there is a galley area with a table and a small fridge, a large stainless-steel coffeepot, and a well-used convection oven, all securely strapped to the bulkheads.

McNamara was a pilot with the call sign "Irish." He asked me how I was enjoying the job. Irish said, "Call me anytime, because this job can kick your ass. It's easy to royally fuck it up."

A serious look came over his face.

"Loop, did you hear he fired his first aide?" he asked.

He asked me if I had double-checked the uniform of the day that the sailors would be wearing when we arrived at Thule so the Admiral would be in the correct uniform. That was an important detail because we always wanted to show up in the right uniform.

"You never want to embarrass the Admiral," McNamara said. I had heard the same from Sam during my turnover. I acknowledged that I had checked every detail of the trip multiple times before our departure.

Irish then asked me, "Did you bring the Admiral's pillow?"

I was puzzled. I had those damn wooden toothpicks, but no pillow.

"A pillow? You're pulling my leg, sir, aren't you?" I asked.

"Nope," Irish said. "Well-known secret for those who have traveled with him. The Admiral always travels with his small personal pillow in a separate navy-blue laundry bag."

"Really?" I was stunned.

"Good ole Sam didn't include that info during the turnover?" Irish asked, looking at me with his balding head, coffee-stained teeth, and bushy eyebrows.

"Sir, you can't be serious," I said.

"Serious as a heart attack," he said. "The Admiral will probably give you a break because it's your first trip, Loop, but he might be pissed."

I did not know what to think. Another officer on the Admiral's staff, Commander Rob Ballard, joined us.

"Hey Rob," Irish said, "New loop here forgot the Admiral's pillow."

"What? He forgot the Admiral's pillow? Oh shit!" Ballard exclaimed.

"Sir, you guys are kidding me, aren't you?" I asked again, hopeful.

"Of all things to forget, you forgot the pillow? Didn't Samuel tell you about that?" Ballard questioned.

This went on for about five minutes. Irish was looking serious and shaking his head. Ballard finally turned away and broke into roaring laughter.

It was indeed good navy humor. No pillow was needed. I started to wonder about those damn wooden toothpicks I had been carrying around for several weeks now.

A FINE NAVY BREAKFAST

Greenland is a beautiful place, but very cold. It was negative ten degrees when we landed in Thule. The sky was overcast. Snow was blowing across the runway. The wind made it feel much colder.

The P-3 squadron was flying in support of a military training exercise with US Navy submarines near the Arctic Circle.

We stayed in military barracks that were built on elevated foundations. Sewer pipes running under the building were insulated and heated so the raw sewage would not freeze on the way out. Long electric cables were available outside most buildings to plug into a cable that extended from the front grills of the cars to keep the batteries from freezing, even during short stops.

Small, skinny arctic foxes freely roamed the base, scurrying around in the snow. The foxes were not bothered by the bitter cold, as they could survive temperatures down to negative 112 Fahrenheit.

Our first morning there, I got up early to preheat our car. Once the Admiral was ready, we drove over the snow-covered roads to the military cafeteria, also known as the galley, to enjoy breakfast with a group of sailors and airmen.

In the military, I could not always count on a galley meal being good. There were some well-known navy classics like "monkey meat on a stick" (meat of unknown origin on a wooden skewer) and "shit on a shingle" or, more commonly, "SOS" (corned beef hash over toast).

However, if I had to bet on a good galley meal, I could bet on breakfast.

We went through the cafeteria line. I got a ham and cheese omelet, bacon, hash browns, toast, a glazed doughnut, coffee, orange juice, and an ice-cold glass of thick chocolate milk from a large stainless-steel dispenser. My metabolism and waistline were much different back then.

The Admiral and I sat with a group of sailors.

"Mind if we join you?" the Admiral asked the young sailors, surprising the hell out of the kids.

After much talk and a lot of "sir, yes, sir" from the sailors, the Admiral finished his meal, downing his last sip of coffee with both hands gripping the coffee cup. He looked around the emptying galley. "Boy, I sure could use a wooden toothpick. You don't happen to see any toothpicks around here, do you?" he asked.

I leaned over and opened my brain. I pulled out an individually wrapped wooden toothpick. I handed it to him.

He grinned. "Nice job, Loop."

"Thank you, Admiral," I replied.

"Sam gave those to you, didn't he?" the Admiral asked as he started working his front teeth with the toothpick.

"Yes, sir, he did."

"Well, thank you for the toothpick. I think you're going to be okay, even though you forgot my pillow. Let's hit the head on the way out," the Admiral said.

"Yes, sir," I said.

At that point, I could have hugged Sam.

I ran into him about two years later and thanked him profusely for the toothpick tip. "Glad it worked out for you," he replied calmly.

Many years later, Sam became the commanding officer of a P-3 squadron.

WHAT I LEARNED

Knowing everything about the Admiral was critical to my success as an aide. The insight about carrying a toothpick and knowing the location of the nearest head were key to a flawlessly executed day. Surely those responsibilities seemed "well below my pay grade." But as odd and seemingly menial as those actions might have been to me, they were essential to the Admiral. If they were important to him, they were important to me. In the navy, we call that "attention to detail."

My breadth of knowledge about the Admiral was extensive. That type of detailed personal knowledge about your boss is rarely expected in the civilian world. That said, the key to your success will be learning about your boss's preferences.

In addition to what your boss tells you, you need to learn all you can from others. Watch, listen, and ask questions of others who have worked with them.

Use all the knowledge you gain about your boss as the foundation for your actions and performance. Don't operate in the blind. Do your homework and research. Know your boss.

Chapter 3

GETTING THINGS DONE

As an Admiral's aide, I learned that there were many different ways to meet the Admiral's expectations or to persuade others to help me when I couldn't do it alone.

To ensure the achievement of his daily goals and my long-term success, I had to use the Admiral's stars many times. As you recall, he told me I could do so in his initial guidance to me.

Most days, however, I did not have to use his stars because I wore an aiguillette.

The aiguillette was a powerful tool in its own right. Its bright-blue-and-gold braid stood out on my uniform. It signaled to all officers the need to be responsive to me as a very young lieutenant, even if they outranked me.

The senior officers I dealt with daily did outrank me. I was the most junior officer on the Admiral's staff, by far. I knew I would likely cross paths with many of them years later without the loop. And they would remember me. It was a small navy, and I was in an even smaller

P-3 community. So I had to be diplomatic and careful when telling them what to do.

On some occasions, however, the loop was not enough. Sometimes I was in uniform and wearing the loop but dealing with someone who did not get it. Other times, when I was in my flight suit or civilian clothes, I did not have the benefit of the loop's visibility.

It was on occasions like these when I needed to use the Admiral's stars.

RENTAL CARS AND UPGRADES

Quite often we flew to Andrews Air Force Base in Washington, DC, for business trips, many times on navy aircraft. I would call the rental car agency in advance so they would have a vehicle parked at Navy Base Operations waiting for us when we landed. I would be the driver. I was specific about the type of car I wanted. Nothing flashy. Nothing with just two doors. Nothing huge. No red sports car. No convertible.

We did not want to be seen in any of those vehicles on official navy business.

"I want a four-door, full-size sedan, preferably in a dark color," I stated when making the reservation. I got to know the rental car clerk in Washington. His name was Ali, and he was a first-generation immigrant and father of five. His English was broken. He was always smiling.

By our fourth trip to Andrews, Ali and I had become friends. On this trip, after we landed and were taxiing up to Base Operations, I looked out the aircraft's window. Ali was standing next to a large, gold, four-door Lincoln Continental. He was enthusiastically giving me two thumbs-up.

Surely that cannot be our car, I thought. Ali jumped in the Lincoln and drove it up to the plane. He popped open the trunk and opened the car doors.

As we walked to the car, the Admiral's displeasure was apparent. Nonetheless, he got into the Lincoln's back seat. I loaded the luggage in the trunk per my normal process (mine first, his second), and got to the driver's side door to shake Ali's hand.

"How do you like your car, Lieutenant Mark?" he asked. "You have been such a good customer and friend; I upgraded you to a fine American-made Lincoln for you and the Admiral."

Not wanting to embarrass Ali, I told him I would call him when we got to our military lodging at the Washington Navy Yard in about thirty minutes. And I asked if he had any other vehicles available.

"Of course we do, Lieutenant Mark. We have many vehicles, but for you and Navy Admiral, today we have the Lincoln," he said, giving me a thumbs-up and a big smile.

Wanting to do us a favor, Ali had upgraded us to a larger vehicle. But he had deviated from my direction. The car resulted in a level of visibility that we did not want—especially when we were staying at the Washington Navy Yard's Visiting Flag Quarters and headed to the Pentagon the next day.

The Visiting Flag Quarters, or VFQ, was the exclusive lodging for flag officers—mostly navy admirals and Marine Corps generals. We stayed there often. As a one-star, the Admiral was typically the lowest-ranking flag officer, as the place was overflowing with three-star admirals. Also, the VFQ was only a few doors down from the official house of the head of the navy, the chief of naval operations.

I got the Admiral to "our" room. At the VFQ, we got a two-bedroom suite. I found that a little awkward at first. I later realized it was just part of the job and getting to know—and see—everything about the Admiral.

GENTLE PERSUASION USING THE STARS

After getting the Admiral situated at the VFQ, I drove back to Andrews. Once there, I told Ali that I wanted a smaller four-door car. He insisted, "Oh no, Lieutenant Mark, you got a complimentary upgrade."

After several unsuccessful attempts to explain that I did not want the upgrade, it was time to use the Admiral's stars. It was getting dark. I had to get another car ASAP and get back to the VFQ for some shuteye.

"Thank you very much, Ali, but the Admiral does not want this car. He is set in his ways. I need another one now."

Looking disappointed, Ali finally said, "Okay, I do what I need to do to make the Admiral happy."

It was late by the time I got the dark blue Ford Taurus back to the Washington Navy Yard. We had an early departure of 0600 the next morning for the Pentagon.

I ran into the VFQ and up the steps to our apartment. As I was turning the corner on the steps, I ran headlong into a tall, muscular man in civilian clothes. He did not budge. He just stared at me. I apologized profusely, knowing that he had to be an admiral.

When I got to the apartment, I told the Admiral I had nearly run over another flag officer. He asked me to describe him. I said, "About six foot four, muscular, tan with blue eyes, short gray hair. He didn't say much."

"That's the head Snake Eater," the Admiral said. "He will be down at breakfast at 0600 eating a bowl of plain oatmeal and a banana."

Snake Eater was the nickname the Admiral used for the navy's exclusive special operations unit, the navy SEALs. In other words, I had run into the top SEAL flag officer.

"You know, he's the real deal. Unlike us P-3 guys, he's a real warrior. He has killed the enemy in combat before," the Admiral said with a slight grimace.

I went to my room, reviewed the schedule for the next day, and fell asleep.

The next morning, as I was leaving the VFQ, I glanced into the small dining area, and indeed, the Snake Eater admiral was there with his oatmeal and a banana.

I walked out and pulled the car around. I parked at the front of the building at 0555, making sure I did not take the closest curbside parking spot.

I stopped the car in front of the sidewalk's exit to avoid blocking any higher-ranking flag officers.

When at the VFQ, I never knew when a three- or four-star might walk out and want to use the sidewalk or have their official black flag transportation SUV pull up. I knew our place, and seniority mattered. I also knew that day that there were quite a few three-stars staying at the VFQ, based on the guest list that I had requested and reviewed in advance.

On cue at 0559, the Admiral walked out of the VFQ. He looked at me, smiled, and winked.

"Good morning, sir," I said as I stood by the open door, popping to attention and giving him a sharp salute.

"Nice car, Loop. Much better. Make sure you tell Ali that I really appreciate this," he said.

As I shut the Admiral's door, I stated, "Aye, aye, sir."

I let the rental car agency manager know that "Ali was the best" and that he always provided exceptional customer service. On future trips, I confirmed with Ali the car type and "no upgrade."

He laughed. "I know that, Lieutenant Mark. You are the only gold customer who does not want to upgrade." I never received an upgrade from Ali again.

MORE DIRECT USE OF THE STARS

There were other times when my use of the stars was more forceful.

For example, I always got our lodging room keys in advance of our arrival. The Admiral did *not* wait in line at the registration desk. I walked him in using the entry door closest to his room, which was typically not the main entrance. If a front-desk clerk refused to give me his room key in advance because they needed to see his ID or it was "against policy," I would explain to the clerk that I was his aide, and I needed the key.

"Look, you don't seem to understand; the Admiral wants his key in advance and has asked me to get it," I would state.

"Sir, we are not allowed to do that per our policy," the clerk might state.

I would then say, "Well, I called in advance and spoke with Ms. Whitman yesterday, and she told me that I would be provided his key. I do not have a lot of time and am trying not to escalate this, but I am prepared to do so. So please give me the key, or call your manager now." I always wrote down names in my handheld "brain" for future reference. I had called ahead and spoken to Ms. Whitman the day before, and she had assured me I would have "no problem" getting his key.

I got the key.

"Thank you very much. I really appreciate your help," I would say with key in hand.

Win gracefully. There was no need to make an enemy, as I might need their help in the future.

I also used the stars to obtain "read-ahead" copies of documents. I might request an advance copy of a brief from the "presentation keeper," who would tell me, "Sir, I cannot give that to you because Commander Burwell told me I could not release it to anyone."

My response would be, "Well, the Admiral is not 'just anyone,' and he wants it in advance. I am confident your chain of command would agree that we need to get it to the Admiral."

I got the read-ahead copy.

"Thank you very much, sir, I really appreciate your help. I know the Admiral does also," I would say. "See you tomorrow!"

I used the stars to get access for my premeeting reconnaissance into various briefing rooms (when access was initially denied). Doing so allowed me to give guidance about how the Admiral preferred the conference room to be set up. Also, I could brief the Admiral on the room's configuration and where he would be seated.

As I said before, it was my job as the loop to know all the details of where we were going before we got there.

WHAT I LEARNED

In the civilian world, I have found many occasions to use my boss's authority and name to get things done. I'm admittedly cautious in doing so. At times, I will tell my boss in advance about the issue I'm working on and that I would like to use their name.

There are multiple ways to accomplish a mission or task. Don't be afraid to diplomatically leverage the resources and names available to you to do so. I do so judiciously as a last resort. You should, too.

A leader knows how and when to play this card without overplaying their hand. Use the stars when you need to. That's what a smart leader does.

Chapter 4

ALWAYS BE ON TIME

One of the most important aspects of my job was to keep the Admiral on time every minute of every day, both in the office and on every trip. As he told me, he did not like to be late.

A WEEK ON THE ROAD

On a weeklong trip, we left Brunswick, Maine, on a Sunday afternoon for a three-day conference at Naval Air Station Moffett Field in California. On the second leg of the trip, we flew from Moffett Field to Naval Air Station Joint Reserve Base New Orleans for a one-day visit. On the last leg of the trip, we were to leave New Orleans at "zero dark thirty" on Friday morning. We needed to be in Jacksonville, Florida, in time for a midmorning change-of-command ceremony at an aviation squadron where the Admiral was just an attendee, not an official participant.

When we left New Orleans Friday morning, the trip had gone spectacularly well so far. I reviewed our agenda for the rest of the day.

By then, all I had to do was get the Admiral to the change of command in the proper uniform at the right time as a guest.

Perhaps because it was Friday and the last stop of a long trip, complacency set in. Complacency is never good. In naval aviation, we say "complacency kills."

We left New Orleans in the early-morning darkness. We were dressed impeccably in our uniforms. The military C-12 aircraft took off on time. The C-12 Huron is a navy dual-propeller Beechcraft Super King Air. We did not have an official arrival party meeting us in Jacksonville, just a young sailor assigned as our driver to take us directly to the squadron hangar where the ceremony was taking place. My schedule had us arriving an hour before the event started.

TIME FOR A LITTLE SHUTEYE

Once airborne, the Admiral took off his shoes and stretched out in his seat. He wanted to get a little more shuteye on the flight. "Make sure you wake me up before we land, Loop," he said. "It's very important to always have your shoes on for landing."

"Aye, aye, sir. Will do," I answered. I set my watch alarm for an hour later. It had been a very long week. The aircraft's air conditioning felt great after the humid New Orleans morning air on the departure tarmac.

We were to land in time for a pre-ceremony VIP reception. The "pre-tea," as we called it, was an opportunity for senior officers, the official party, and the commanding officer's family to gather before the formal ceremony. At the pre-tea, sailors in dress uniforms would serve nonalcoholic drinks from a bubbling sterling fountain that was passed around between the commands for these events. There were usually some small appetizers. It was held in the ready room or officers' wardroom in the squadron hangar.

About an hour later, I heard the beeping of my watch. We were about thirty minutes from arrival when the Admiral woke up. He put his shoes on.

WHAT TIME IS THE PRE-TEA?

"Hey, Loop, what time does the pre-tea start?" he asked.

"It starts at 0900, Admiral. The change of command is at ten hundred," I said.

He looked at his watch. He looked back at me. "You sure?" he asked. "Because it is approaching nine thirty right now."

The Admiral gazed at me with raised eyebrows and that "something's not right" look.

Oh shit, I thought.

I felt sick when I realized what had happened. I had not accounted for the one-hour time difference between central time in New Orleans and eastern time in Jacksonville.

That was an egregious error.

The Admiral remained quiet for the rest of the flight. It was a very long thirty minutes!

We landed around 0955. A young sailor pulled up to the aircraft in a white military vehicle. The yardarm with the Admiral's flag was flying on the front bumper. He saluted as he opened the passenger-side rear door for the Admiral to get in.

"Good morning, Admiral. We're glad you made it, sir." The sailor in his dress white crackerjack uniform had been sitting there for over an hour waiting for us.

"Thank you, shipmate. I am very sorry we are late," the Admiral said. When we arrived at the hangar, we sheepishly walked to one of the last rows of chairs, raising a few eyebrows, and found seats in the very back of the hangar.

After the ceremony, at the reception at the officers' club, the new commanding officer said to the Admiral, "Sir, I am glad you made it. I didn't see you at the pre-tea and was worried you had missed your flight."

"Skipper, sorry we were late," the Admiral said. "We had a slight scheduling snafu, but the loop here always takes care of me. I would not have missed this for the world!"

We left the reception in about an hour to catch our departing flight.

"Don't let that happen again, Mark," the Admiral said to me in the car after we left the reception.

And I didn't.

In the navy, we often said, "One 'aw, shit,' can wipe out a string of 'attaboys.'" That was definitely an "aw, shit!"

SPAIN TO FLORIDA ON A P-3

On one of our overseas trips, we were flying from Rota, Spain, back to Naval Air Station Jacksonville on a squadron P-3. We flew on squadron P-3s often.

We had strong headwinds at the start of the flight, as is often the case on a westerly flight from Europe back to the US. Based on our ground speed, I calculated our arrival time at NAS Jacksonville to be 1500. I asked the aircrew to communicate that arrival time to those at our home base and in Jacksonville.

I told the lead pilot, the patrol plane commander or PPC, that 1500 was the exact time that I wanted the Admiral to step off the airplane and for them to fly the plane accordingly.

I continued to monitor our estimated time of arrival as we made our way across the Atlantic.

Halfway across the Atlantic Ocean, the headwinds died down, and our ground speed was increasing. I knew our ETA was creeping up earlier than 1500.

The Admiral already had a few hours at the stick and was snoozing in the TACCO seat in the aircraft's back end, or "tube." The TACCO seat was where the tactical aircraft coordinator sat and directed the crew's operations when the aircraft was flying a tactical mission. It was on the port side behind the cockpit. On a transit flight that was not an operational mission, the crew usually designated the TACCO seat as the VIP seat.

Across from that seat was where the navigator communicator, or NAVCOM, sat. In front of both forward-facing seats was a wall of electronics, flight instruments, gauges, and switches.

I went into the cockpit. The plane was on autopilot. The copilot was reading the newspaper. The pilot who was "flying the plane" was chatting with the middle-seat flight engineer, or FE.

"Sir, as I said earlier, the Admiral needs to step off the plane exactly at 1500. If you could please adjust our airspeed accordingly," I reiterated.

"Yeah, we got it," the PPC said. He quickly returned to his conversation with the FE about Florida college football.

I went back to my seat in the tube. I dozed off for a while, not fully sleeping because I never slept on the job as a loop.

About an hour later, I calculated our arrival time again. To my dismay, we were heading for an arrival about thirty minutes earlier than what I had requested.

Damn it!

SLOW THIS BUS DOWN

I knew a three-star admiral who was an old friend of the Admiral was going to meet us when we landed. I also knew that the three-star's loop was counting on our exact arrival time. Getting there early would be a disaster because my boss would have to wait around for thirty minutes for the senior admiral to arrive. Then, when the three-star did arrive, it would be an embarrassing situation for both of them.

As you recall, Sam and Irish had warned me never to embarrass the Admiral.

By now, the Admiral was awake. He looked at his watch. We were thinking the same thing. I was running out of time. At this point, I no longer had the time to be cordial.

Time to use the stars to make sure we were on time.

I glanced up at the Admiral as I walked up to the cockpit.

A LITTLE EXTRA STICK AND RUDDER

I tapped the PPC on the shoulder and said, "Sir, just to be clear, the Admiral wants to step foot on the ground exactly at 1500. If that does not happen, the Admiral will be upset, a three-star admiral will be upset, and when I explain the situation to your commanding officer, he's going to be upset. Shit's going to roll downhill quickly to you as the PPC. I really need your help here, sir."

My volume caught the attention of the PPC, the copilot, and the senior enlisted FE.

The PPC said, "Mark, we were just trying to make up some time to get you there early."

I stated: "Sir, there's no need to make up any time because the only time that matters is our exact arrival time at 1500. Now, I'm going to leave the cockpit and let you gentlemen execute accordingly. When I go back in the tube, the Admiral will ask me 'We gonna be on time?' and I will respond with 'yes, sir.'"

At this point, I knew these pilots, who were senior to me, were thinking crude thoughts about me. However, I could not worry about hurt feelings. They would realize later I was doing them a big favor.

As I left the cockpit to return to my seat, I felt the aircraft decelerate. In the P-3, with its four large turboprop engines, you could feel and hear when the plane accelerated or decelerated based on inertial movement and the humming sound of its four turboprop engines.

As I walked back by the Admiral, he leaned over to me and said, "How's it looking, Loop? We gonna be on time?"

I stated, "Yes, sir."

He grinned and said, "You told them to slow down, didn't you?" He winked.

The Admiral was a P-3 pilot with thousands of flight hours. He could guess our true airspeed just by the engines' hum.

I smiled.

At 1452, we flew over the beautiful St. Johns River at the end of the NAS Jax runway, and the wheels hit the deck at about 1454.

As we were taxiing in, I stuck my head in the cockpit and shook the hands of the two pilots and the FE.

"Thank you, commander, great job. Sure appreciate the lift, and we'll pass that along to your skipper," I said.

I needed to do my best to leave on good terms with these pilots because I never knew when I would see them again in the future without the protection of the loop. They were senior to me and would remember me.

I went to the back of the tube to pre-position our luggage near the door.

After a slow taxi, we pulled up to the VIP parking spot at the air terminal at 1457. The engines shut down. The Admiral stuck his head in the cockpit and thanked the pilots and FE.

The aircrew lowered the P-3 aircraft ladder, and the Admiral's foot hit the deck at 1500.

The three-star admiral was there. He had arrived five minutes earlier at 1455.

THE THANK-YOU NOTE

The Admiral always sent thank-you letters after every trip. On our trips, I kept track of the names of those who should receive one from him.

About ten days later, the flight crew's commanding officer received a personal note from the Admiral on his official letterhead. I knew that the CO would share that note with those named in it.

I wrote that thank-you letter, as I did for many dozens of others. It went like this:

> *Dear Skipper Sampson,*
>
> *I wanted to thank you for the recent ride from Rota to Jacksonville on October 28th. The professionalism and pride of your crew was clearly evident, and that is a tribute to your outstanding leadership.*
>
> *In particular, I wanted to thank AW1 Dewberry for the exceptional hosting. Additionally, LCDR Eberson, LCDR Peterson, and ADCS Alexander did a phenomenal job getting us there safely and on time—down to the minute! Bravo Zulu to the Pelican crew for a job well done! I'll fly with your team anytime!*
>
> *Respectfully,*
> *The Admiral*

WHAT I LEARNED

It is important to be on time. As an aviator and a lawyer, being punctual is critical. As a naval aviator, not being on time can get you killed.

As a lawyer, being late with a legal response can be legal malpractice. As a leader, those who are watching you are also watching the clock. Finally, as a follower, your boss is paying attention to your ability to be on time and meet deadlines.

If you are an aspiring young professional, your supervisors will notice if you're consistently late to meetings or missing deadlines. Don't be that person!

If you are the leader, your followers will not appreciate your being late. While it's unlikely anyone will tell you, as the leader, that your reputation is being tarnished by your tardiness, it is. People depend on your timing. They get there in advance of your arrival to wait for you. If you are late, you keep everyone waiting. Keeping others waiting for you and always being late is inconsiderate.

Today, if I am running late, I call or text others to tell them so and apologize. Being late happens, but it should be the exception to a consistent pattern of being on time.

If you want to be seen as a leader and get promoted, you should meet deadlines and always be punctual.

Chapter 5

WORKPLACE CONFIDENTIALITY AND DISCRETION

When I became an admiral's aide, the Admiral told me that confidentiality mattered.

The confidentiality rule applied to what I saw when in uniform and to what the Admiral did in his free time. I knew what he did every minute of the day.

The Admiral was a kind man, but what he did after hours with his family was his own business and not for me to share.

"Scuttlebutt" is a navy term for gossip. The term originated in the 1800s in that the cask carrying a ship's daily supply of fresh water was referred to as a scuttlebutt. The term carried over to the water fountain on a ship or in a navy facility. Today we call it "water cooler gossip."

I'm also reminded that years ago, the navy had a famous wartime slogan: "Loose lips sink ships."

One beautiful Saturday afternoon when we were preparing to leave for a two-week trip the following Monday, I went by the navy base barbershop.

By then, the Admiral had told me several times that I probably wasn't going to be fired. That was reassuring because I knew that the Admiral *had* fired his first aide. I wasn't sure why, but I would learn later.

JACK THE BARBER

I was in civilian clothes that day when I went to the barbershop, but Jack the barber knew me. I visited him weekly. I always had to look "inspection ready" in uniform, and that included a regulation haircut. He had been cutting hair there for years. There was only one admiral in Brunswick, so everyone knew him and his family. They all recognized me, too, as the Admiral's aide.

Once I was in the chair, we proceeded to talk about the weather, what we had planned for the rest of the week, and several other topics, most of which were pure scuttlebutt. I told him that our travel schedule had been hectic and that we were headed back out of town Monday. I also told Jack that I was going over to the Admiral's house that evening for an informal wedding ceremony for one of the Admiral's senior enlisted staff members. That interested him.

The wedding was a private ceremony for the flag writer senior chief. She was "front-office family," like me. She had been with the Admiral from the beginning. She was marrying another senior enlisted member of the Admiral's staff, and the Admiral had invited a small group to his quarters to witness the ceremony.

I went to the simple wedding ceremony on Saturday evening at his official quarters.

I spent Sunday going to church, resting, packing, and studying our travel itinerary.

On Monday morning at 0600, I picked up the Admiral at his quarters in the official sedan to drive to the squadron hangar for a P-3 departure.

When he got in the car, he said, "Good morning, Loop. How was the rest of your weekend?"

"It was great, Admiral. Thank you for asking," I said.

"I see you got your hair cut by Jack on Saturday," he said.

While it might have been obvious that I had gotten a haircut, I was unsure how the Admiral knew that Jack had done it.

He got right to the point. "Well, I got my hair cut by Jack on Sunday. He gives a good haircut, doesn't he?" the Admiral stated.

"Yes, sir, he does," I said.

The Admiral continued. "Jack's a good guy. I've been going to him for over a year now. But he can be a little chatty."

"Yes, sir," I said.

"He asked me how the wedding was at my quarters Saturday night. That was none of his business." The Admiral paused. "You see where I'm coming from?" he asked.

"Sir, yes, sir," I stated.

"You see, Lieutenant," he said—when he called me Lieutenant rather than Loop, I knew it was a "foot-stomper" teaching moment, and likely I had screwed something up—"what we do when wearing the uniform is official business and nobody else's business. What I do after hours is personal business and also nobody else's business. Be sure to keep it that way."

"Yes, sir. I'm very sorry. It won't happen again." And it did not. I kept my mouth shut about his business. No scuttlebutt!

A CONGRESSIONAL ENCOUNTER

On another Maine summer morning, the Admiral called me into his office.

"Loop, close the door," he said.

When he said "close the door," he wanted my undivided attention on a sensitive matter.

"If the weather holds up this week, we are having a VIP fly in on Friday. He will want a short tour of the base. After that, we're going to put my boat on the Androscoggin River and go fishing for the day. Accompanying the VIP will be another admiral. He's a great friend of mine and is going places. It is very important to me, personally, that this day goes well. Any questions?"

"No, sir, not really," I said.

THE PLAN FOR A FISHING TRIP

"You're not going fishing with us, but you're going to be there. You're going to drive the VIP and the other admiral to the dock, and I'm going to pull up in my boat and take them fishing. You will sit on the dock with the brick in case we need anything. Any questions?"

The "brick" was a large black walkie-talkie. It was the size of a red brick. We did not have iPhones or even flip phones back then.

"No, sir. I got it, Admiral. You want me to be a dock boy for the day. No problem. I can do that, sir," I said.

"Good. Now I need you to find some Clamato juice before Friday morning. Buy two or three bottles, some big red cups, and a couple of bags of ice. This should cover it," the Admiral stated as he slapped two twenty-dollar bills in my hand.

I had no idea what Clamato juice was. I found it at the local grocery store that evening. It was tomato juice mixed with spices and dried clam broth. It tasted a lot like a seafood Bloody Mary mix. It was pretty good! I know because I bought a fourth bottle and tried it with a little vodka that night.

That Thursday morning, the Admiral got confirmation that the trip was going forward. He called me into his office again.

"Close the door," he said.

THE CONGRESSMAN

"Now, Loop. The congressman is a navy veteran, a longtime friend of the navy, and a truly great American. Doctors have recently diagnosed him with cancer. We want him to have a good day."

He was coming to Brunswick with the one-star navy chief of legislative affairs. The navy selected only the most polished admirals to be its representatives on Capitol Hill.

When Friday morning came, it was a picture-perfect day. We met the congressman and the congressional admiral when their aircraft landed on base. I quickly drove them over to the wing commander headquarters building on base. There in a large conference room, the senior navy staff gave them a short dog-and-pony presentation. We then provided a "windshield tour" of the base, driving along a predesignated route.

The briefing and the tour were completed in about an hour.

OFF TO THE RIVER

Fishing was next! We ended the tour at the base bachelor officer quarters, or BOQ. That is the on-base hotel for officers. I had reserved two VIP suites so the congressman and visiting admiral could change into fishing clothes. While they did so, I ran down the hall and changed in the lobby head. I was waiting outside their doors before either one of them came out. As I have said before, never keep an admiral waiting—or a congressman.

The congressman came out of his room with a fishing hat and vest.

I then drove the congressman and the congressional admiral about thirty minutes away to the dock on the Androscoggin River. I had driven there the day before, so I knew exactly where it was.

The Androscoggin is a river with clear, cold, rushing water and rocky shores in some areas. Tall evergreen trees hover over the bank. Fishing guides describe the river as being good for prize-winning rainbow and brown trout.

That day, the air was cool. The water was cold. The sun was shining, and the sky was clear. When we arrived at the dock on time, I could see the Admiral a couple of hundred yards away in his boat, motoring toward us. When the Admiral moored to the dock, I helped the congressman and visiting admiral get in the boat.

Fishing rods, bait, and a cooler with Clamato juice on ice were already in the boat, along with some wrapped deli sandwiches. Off they went, disappearing around a bend.

I sat there for quite a while, fighting the urge to drift off to sleep and waving away a few black flies.

After about two hours, I saw the boat laboring back up the river against the current, headed toward the dock.

"Hey, Mark, we're coming back for a quick break," the Admiral said over the brick.

"Roger that, sir," I acknowledged. "Standing by."

Once again, I assisted with the docking of the boat. Once it was secured, the Admiral handed me a small trash bag and then a plastic male handheld urinal. It was full. I didn't say a word.

I stepped to the side of the dock, dumped the urinal in the river, and rinsed it out. I shook it off and handed it back to the Admiral.

They hadn't caught any fish, but they headed back out, determined to keep trying.

THE STORM

About twenty minutes later, I saw the boat racing back toward the pier. A cluster of dark clouds was rolling toward us over the trees. The sky opened up with hard rain, and the temperature dropped twenty degrees.

I helped secure the boat as the Admiral steered it alongside. We had not anticipated the rain, nor did we have any foul-weather gear, so everybody was soaked. We decided to call it a day.

I got the congressman and the visiting admiral back into the car. The Admiral left the dock to take his boat back to the boat ramp. Even though the fishing excursion had been unsuccessful and was cut short by several hours, the visiting admiral and the congressman were in fine spirits.

DOING LAUNDRY

Other than the suit he had on when he arrived, the congressman did not have any dry clothes. Having cut the fishing trip short, we had a couple of hours to kill before his departure flight.

When we got back to the BOQ, we walked the congressman to his room. The visiting admiral said, "Congressman, you go take a hot shower, but first, hand me your wet clothes through the door. We'll take care of them."

As I stood next to the visiting admiral at the congressman's door, it cracked open just a few inches. Out came the congressman's hand with a ball of wet clothes—socks, skivvies, T-shirt, and all. They were placed right into the hands of a navy admiral.

I resisted the urge to laugh as I realized we were going to wash and dry the congressman's clothes, including his white T-shirt and underwear. There was a laundry room down the hall. I went to the front desk and bought a small box of Tide for a quarter.

About an hour and a half later, we delivered a neatly folded, warm, dry stack of clothes to the congressman's room.

They left later that afternoon. I knew that despite the rainstorm and the unsuccessful fishing trip, the congressman had enjoyed the time. Just getting out of Washington, DC, and on the Androscoggin was therapeutic. Mission accomplished!

THE REST OF THE STORY

A few weeks later, I received a personal thank-you note from the congressional admiral. Years later, he went on to earn three more stars. He retired as a four-star.

Later that year, the congressman passed away, and thousands attended his funeral.

WHAT I LEARNED

Other than my wife and parents, I never told anyone about being a dock boy that day as a young navy lieutenant. It's been over thirty years now. The congressman and the visiting admiral were able to get in and out of town without any visibility. While lawyers had approved the trip, it was no one else's business.

The barbershop episode and the congressman's trip reinforced the importance of confidentiality. I learned from the Admiral the importance of keeping matters discussed at work and about one's personal life private. That information is usually nobody else's business. This is true when dealing with your colleagues and your boss.

Many times, the personal and professional business you learn at work should not be a topic of discussion at the barbershop, around the water cooler, or as you are passing the mashed potatoes at the family dinner table. Be thoughtful about what you share.

Scuttlebutt can spread quickly. Leaders are wise and discrete. It's best not to engage in scuttlebutt.

Chapter 6

KNOW ALL THE DETAILS

As an admiral's aide, knowing all the details concerning the Admiral's transportation was critical to my daily success.

A five-day trip could involve ten to fifteen different transportation modes, including military and commercial planes, trains, automobiles, ferries, rental cars, official navy vehicles, and private sedans. I had to confirm and reconfirm all reservations. Punctuality was critical. I could not lose luggage or briefcases. I could not be late.

When I was driving, I needed to know the route cold. I did so with verbal directions and highlighted paper maps. If I had the time, I would drive the route in advance, because you never knew when road construction might be ongoing. Doing so also allowed me to time the travel. This was long before Waze or even a first-generation car GPS that plugged into the cigarette lighter.

Transportation introduced a level of uncertainty and risk over which I had little control.

A HELICOPTER AND SUMMER WHITES

About six months into the job, the Admiral finally told me why he'd fired his first aide. It involved an international trip in which his aide was coordinating a visit with the Japanese navy. The plan was for the Admiral to fly out on a Japanese helicopter to a small Japanese navy frigate that was underway about a hundred miles offshore in the Pacific Ocean. They were going to meet a Japanese admiral on board that "small boy."

"Admiral, you'll take the helicopter out to the destroyer for your visit with the Japanese admiral and crew," the aide had briefed the Admiral before the trip. "You'll be on board for about two hours."

The Admiral wore his summer whites for the trip, a beautiful white uniform with black-and-gold shoulder boards. His gold pilot wings and a colorful rack of military ribbons were neatly pinned a quarter inch above his left pocket, and his nametag was a quarter inch above his right pocket.

We called that uniform the Good Humor Ice Cream Man uniform because the complete outfit—with its white belt, white socks, white cover, and matching white shoes—made the wearer look like the old-fashioned Good Humor Ice Cream Man. (For the younger generation, Google that, and you'll understand.) That said, it was a fine uniform that made for an impressive "An Officer and a Gentleman" appearance.

As the Admiral told me, after a lot of handshaking and bowing when they arrived at the Japanese navy base, he boarded the Japanese military helicopter and was off over the blue ocean headed to the ship. When the ship came into view, the Admiral gazed down at it.

IS THAT THE RIGHT BOAT?

That's odd, he thought, recognizing that the ship did not have a helicopter landing pad on the stern.

The helicopter began a circling descent. The Admiral pointed to the ship and looked to the Japanese aircrew, who gave him a thumbs-up.

The aircrew began assembling a body harness to lower the Admiral by cable to the ship. The harness straps would wrap tightly in between his legs and around his crotch and connect with a large buckle securely across his chest. Attached to the chest strap was a metal D-ring which the crew would attach to the helicopter's lift cable.

The Admiral told me that at that point, there was nothing he could do but to go along with the plan. However, this was very embarrassing, and as I have said before, an aide never embarrasses his admiral.

With the aircrew's help, the Admiral strapped into the harness in his summer white uniform with chest ribbons and military insignia straining, and the straps permanently discoloring his white uniform around his crotch.

The aide had assumed that the transfer via helicopter to the ship would include landing onboard the ship. This was an honest mistake, but you never assumed anything as an aide.

Years later, as the Admiral told me that story over a beer after a long day, he was laughing so hard that he had to wipe his eyes. I laughed to tears also, knowing this could have happened to me. Unfortunately for my predecessor, that was strike one! Strike two would come the very next day—and there was no strike three in this job.

CHECKING OUT OF LODGING

The Admiral continued telling me the story.

The next morning, they were checking out of the hotel before sunrise. That evening, the Admiral had told his first aide, "Don't pay the bill until we are both out of the rooms tomorrow morning." The

Admiral knew the aide always paid the lodging bill in advance of their departure so as not to keep the Admiral waiting. The departure was to be efficient, taking the Admiral directly from the room to the waiting vehicle without stopping at the front desk.

The Admiral also knew that at this hotel, the front-desk attendant would turn off the master power switch to the room as soon as the aide paid the bill. Without power, the room would be dark.

The Admiral got up early the next day. He began the standard Navy morning routine, "three S's," two of which were a shower and a shave. While he was still on the toilet in the windowless bathroom, all the lights in the room went out with an audible *ker-chunk*. He knew exactly what had happened. All he could do was yell out at the top of his lungs, "LIEU-TEN-ANT!"

The aide had made it down the hall to the Admiral's room door just in time for the front-desk clerk to secure the power to the room. He had forgotten the Admiral's direction and had paid the bill.

Hearing the Admiral belt out his name from inside the room, all the aide could do was yell back instinctively, "Yes, sir, Admiral."

That was strike two—the end of the first aide.

After a man-to-man discussion with the Admiral when they got back to the continental United States, they agreed things were just not working out. The Admiral and the aide came to a mutual agreement. They decided that neither one of them was enjoying their jobs. The lieutenant just was not cut out to be a loop.

The Admiral took care of him, though. He made sure he got orders to a competitive job at a good duty station. Nowhere in his written military fitness report was there any indication that the Admiral had relieved him. On review of those records, one would assume he had just performed a temporary duty assignment on the Admiral's staff en route to a permanent shore duty assignment.

I heard that he was a superstar at his next duty station and enjoyed a successful career, unblemished by his failure as an aide.

WHAT I LEARNED

Details matter not only in the military, but also in any profession. With advance planning, you can be prepared with all the facts and details. You should know the facts better than your colleagues or opponent, whether in a conference room or the courtroom. You also need to know the facts better than your boss.

Preparation is key to successful execution. Not knowing all the details in a detail-oriented business can result in you not looking like a leader.

I also learned that good bosses demonstrate grace, empathy, and compassion. They will allow you to make mistakes and will have that hard discussion with you when it is necessary. Great bosses will allow failure and allow you to learn from failure. Exceptional bosses will take care of those who fail and allow them an opportunity to recover.

The Admiral was an exceptional boss.

Chapter 7

CHECK THE DETAILS

As an admiral's aide, I was responsible for ensuring that the Admiral's speeches were well written, appropriately targeted for the audience, and properly positioned on the podium of the stage where he would be speaking.

The timing for positioning the Admiral's speech at any event was a challenge. The Admiral was prone to editing his paper copy with a red pen just hours before his speech. Late edits made my job difficult, but not impossible. I became very good at flawlessly executing the difficult.

SPEECH PREPARATION

When the Admiral was a guest speaker at any event, the enlisted senior chief flag writer and I drafted the speech weeks in advance. The Admiral trusted us to write the speech in his voice. We wrote and revised it with the help of the staff public affairs officer, or PAO.

The Admiral saw the speech briefly a couple of times before the event. We would make all revisions as he requested. Hours before the event, he would study the speech in the car on the way to the event or in a quiet holding room before it began.

THE SPLENDOR OF A NAVY CHANGE-OF-COMMAND CEREMONY

A navy change of command is an impressive ceremony, steeped in tradition. It includes a lot of pomp and circumstance in full dress uniforms, the American flag, all the troops standing in formation in inspection-ready uniforms, and a navy band playing ceremonial music.

The formal ceremony marks the passing of command authority from one officer to another. The ceremony usually occurs on a large stage or on the ship's deck. The outgoing CO and the incoming CO, along with their boss, the navy chaplain, and a guest speaker, make up the official party. The passing of authority occurs with hand salutes and the words exchanged by the incoming CO: "I relieve you, sir," and the outgoing CO: "I stand relieved!"

I planned, executed, and participated in many of them in the navy.

THE CHANGE-OF-COMMAND SPEECH SHUFFLE

One summer day we flew to Jacksonville, Florida, when the Admiral was scheduled to be the guest speaker at a change of command for one of his P-3 squadrons.

For that ceremony, we were wearing our full dress choker white uniforms. That uniform is all white, with a high neck collar, large medals, white gloves, and the ceremonial navy officer's sword. As I expected, the Admiral edited his paper copy of the speech within an hour of the ceremony's start time.

We had a system to make sure the speech went as planned. I had to protect the speech. Back then—over thirty years ago—it was not uncommon for the squadron's unofficial "Junior Officer Protection Association," called JOPA, to remove a page of the speech from the binder and insert the latest pinup centerfold. Or they might replace the water in the glass sitting near his chair on the official dais with 100 percent pure grain clear alcohol. Sipping from that glass made for an unpleasant surprise on a blazingly humid Jacksonville day while sweating profusely in a polyester high-collared white dress uniform.

As the guests began filling the seats that faced the red, white, and blue stage on the squadron hangar deck, I checked my watch. We were twenty minutes from the ceremony's commencement. They all start on time. The Admiral handed me his marked-up copy of the speech. I raced to the squadron's administrative office to make two copies of it.

I knew the photocopy machine had been working that morning because I had gone by the administrative office as soon as I had dropped the Admiral off at the room where the VIP guests were meeting with close family and friends for the pre-tea. I told the young petty officer sitting closest to the copy machine to secure the machine and make sure no one was using it thirty minutes before the ceremony. This plan depended on the photocopy machine being "free and clear" and working that day, which was always a risk.

I hastily made two copies of the original.

When I returned with the copies, the Admiral was lining up with the official party to prepare to walk to the stage. I helped him secure his navy sword to his sword belt. I gave him his white gloves. I handed him the folded original. I updated him as to the other flag officers or official guests who had showed up without being on the RSVP list—so he could acknowledge them in his opening remarks—as well as those who had not arrived after all.

I walked downstairs in the hangar to where the ceremonial stage and several hundred white folding chairs had been set up. The guests were already seated. The squadron was standing in formation behind the rows of chairs.

Once there, I inserted a copy of his speech, page by page, into the master program and speech binder. I was finished about ten minutes before the ceremony began. I placed the binder on the podium.

I kept the second copy with me. Using this process, we were always prepared for contingencies. If the Admiral got to the podium, and the speech was missing from the binder, he had the original in his pocket that he could pull out. And I had the second copy as a backup that I could always pass up to him, although doing so would have been the last resort.

As this ceremony began, I was sitting in the third row behind the commanding officer's family, almost directly in front of the podium.

As a loop, I always kept a line of sight to the Admiral wherever we were. "Losing" him was not a good thing. It was always humorous at a large conference full of flag officers for a colleague loop to run around the corner and ask, "Have you seen my admiral?" We all knew that an admiral on the loose could be a challenge.

More entertaining would be when an admiral rounded the corner and bumped into a bunch of loops waiting on their bosses. We would pop to attention, and the admiral would ask, "Hey, any of you seen my loop?" Not good.

PAGE TWELVE

On the stage, after the invocation, the Admiral began his speech by greeting the CO's family and special guests. He was halfway into the speech when he turned the page at the podium and took a slight pause. He began going off the transcript. I knew the speech by heart. The flag writer and I had written it, and I had rehearsed it by reading it out loud at his pace to make sure I got the timing right—twenty-one minutes, to be exact.

He glanced at me from the elevated stage.

After a minute, he returned to the prepared remarks.

When the ceremony ended with the chaplain's benediction and the retiring of the colors, the official party left the stage. The band blasted the traditional navy song "Anchors Aweigh."

I made my way to the Admiral's side to retrieve his navy sword, his cover, and his white gloves.

An officer approached the Admiral and stated, "Admiral, I sure enjoyed your speech! It was perfect for the occasion!"

"Well, thank you, I always appreciate hearing that." The Admiral grinned. "The loop here helped me a lot with it."

More folks came up to compliment the Admiral. In between the small talk, he leaned over to me and asked, "How did I do?" He would always ask me that after a speech.

I stated, "Sir, you did good, even though it appeared around the middle of the speech you lost your place just for a few seconds. I don't think anyone else noticed."

"I did, Lieutenant," he said. "The speech was missing page twelve. Don't ever let that happen again. Always make sure you page-check my documents."

"Yes, sir, it won't happen again," I stated.

And it never did.

WHAT I LEARNED

Fast forward to about ten years ago in my corporate legal job. I was helping the general counsel of my multibillion-dollar employer prepare for a public speech that the national press was covering. He had flown into Charleston, South Carolina, from Chicago.

He was editing his speech minutes before he was to give it, much like the Admiral used to do years before. My exceptional administrative assistant, Patty, was making the edits and reprinting the speech. When we printed the last edits, I retrieved the speech from the printer and put the speech page by page in a three-ring binder.

I handed the binder to the general counsel.

He looked at me and asked, "All the changes made correctly?"

"Yes, sir," I said.

"Are you sure?" he asked.

"Yes, sir," I said.

"Did you page-check it?" he asked.

"Yes, sir, I did," I said.

"Are you willing to bet your job on that?" he asked.

"Yes, sir," I said with a nod.

I had been page-checking documents for twenty-five years.

To this day, I always page-check every document I copy or scan. I did that as a litigation partner when filing documents with the court and still do so as an in-house corporate attorney. I also insist that page numbers are visible on every page as I count the pages.

I exercise the same care with all my presentations. Before I give a presentation or speak to a large audience, I go to the presentation room and run the presentation on the exact equipment I will be using, making sure every page advances properly and any video executes on cue at the right volume. I also test the microphone and the handheld PowerPoint clicker.

There is nothing more embarrassing than being onstage before a large audience or pitching in a small conference room to a bunch of senior executives, and your presentation doesn't work.

Check everything in advance. This allows you the time to adjust your presentation, if necessary. Then you appear confident and polished in your speech. You look like a leader.

Chapter 8

CREATE SIMPLE HABITS TO STAY ORGANIZED

As an admiral's aide, travel was fast and furious. People and luggage could start moving very quickly when transferring from a plane to a vehicle.

I never lost sight of the Admiral, and I never lost sight of his luggage, briefcase, and personal items. I hand-carried his personal ceremonial US Navy officer's sword that he'd had for over thirty years. I guarded his belongings with a passion.

After any arrival, I made sure that our luggage stayed with us. I could not lose any of his stuff or have someone mistakenly place it in the wrong vehicle. I could not allow anyone to do that with my luggage either, because the schedule would never have allowed me to leave the Admiral to look for my luggage.

COUNT AND RECOUNT

I developed a simple process to make sure we never lost any of our bags. I counted the number of items we had on every trip. On most trips, between the two of us, we had two pieces of Rollaboard luggage, two briefcases, two hanging bags, and one sword case. Seven items.

I visually counted them at every opportunity. I counted them when I packed the car before departure. I counted them when I got out of the car to get on the aircraft. I counted them when I was on the aircraft before the car drove off. I counted them upon arrival at our destination when we got off the plane. I counted them when I packed them in the car's trunk. Finally, I counted them when I took them out of the car at our lodging.

This fail-safe technique always worked. One time, when we got on a plane to leave after a squadron ceremony, I counted only six pieces. *Holy shit*, I thought. *Where's his sword?* We had left it in the back seat of the car. I ran off the plane and got it.

When flying on military aircraft into military bases, the welcoming group would position our white navy sedan near the parked plane and at the front of the line, if there were multiple cars.

As soon as we got off the plane, the Admiral would do the back-slapping and grip and grinning with the welcoming party. I had my eyes locked on our luggage. I kept it separated from all other bags. I refused to let anyone else touch it—other than perhaps to briefly carry it off the plane. When we flew on a squadron P-3, we carried all our luggage on the plane, storing it near the aircraft door. The crew secured it with a large green cargo net. Our luggage was always last on and first off.

Many times, on the tarmac, some well-intentioned greeter would say, "Admiral, I got your bags," to which I would have to interject, "Thank you very much, but I will take care of them."

Thinking they were doing me a favor, at times the greeter persisted: "Oh, that's okay, Lieutenant. I'll take the bags."

"No, thank you, but I got the Admiral's bags. I just need the room keys," I would say.

"No problem, Lieutenant. It's okay. I can get those for you." The greeter would continue, "Here are the keys."

Time to use the Admiral's stars.

"Thank you for the keys. I got the Admiral's bags. He prefers it that way," I would reiterate as I grabbed his bags.

LUGGAGE LOGISTICS

I packed the bags in the car's trunk in a matter of minutes, so the car was loaded before the Admiral was ready to get in. I was purposeful in doing so.

The order in which I put them into the trunk determined how they would come out of the trunk. First in, last out. This was essential for a smooth arrival at our lodging. Again, always think ahead.

I put our Rollaboard luggage in first. I put his briefcase on top of his Rollaboard. I draped our hanging bags over the top of the briefcases. I laid the Admiral's sword case on top of the hanging bags, making sure that it was clear of the trunk's hinges. If I was in doubt, I put the sword in the car's back seat. I shut the trunk and stood by his open door.

With the car loaded and the room keys in my right pocket, he could jump in the car as soon as he was ready, and off we went. When we pulled up to our military lodging, I took the bags out in order. We walked directly to his room with the room key in my hand.

WHAT I LEARNED

I discuss the intricacies of packing luggage in the trunk of a car as an example of paying attention to details and creating simple, fail-safe organizational habits. We traveled around the world, and I never lost our luggage because I was always counting it. I was always thinking ahead so that the way I put the luggage in the trunk made sense fifteen minutes later when I took it out.

My luggage-counting habit is an old one. Old habits are hard to break. On my family's prepandemic weeklong vacation from Charleston to Paris with my lovely wife and three beautiful daughters, we had fourteen pieces of carry-on and checked luggage between us. I know because I counted. The ladies packed a lot of shoes for Paris!

When we landed at Charles de Gaulle Airport, we got off the plane without leaving any carry-on items. I had counted them again. At the chaotic international arrival baggage claim carousel, I started to retrieve our bags one by one.

When my oldest daughter tried to help me get the luggage from the baggage carousel, I was in the process of counting the bags. I snapped at her, "Go stand with your mother. I got this!" I apologized to her later. However, I successfully got all fourteen items, including purses, backpacks, and suitcases, from our home in Charleston to the two hotel rooms in downtown Paris.

Good leaders are also always thinking ahead. A good leader needs to look and be organized.

Chapter 9

ASK FOR HELP WHEN YOU NEED IT

My success as an Admiral's aide depended on many things, one of which was to know when to ask for help.

As a loop, I could not get lost.

I was also not supposed to stop to ask for directions along the way unless it was absolutely necessary. When going places, the Admiral followed my lead. He was walking with me quickly, either right beside me or slightly behind me. We walked to a destination with confidence and precision.

THE SHIP

As a young naval flight officer, or NFO, the only evolution for me worse than navigating the Pentagon with its miles of hallways was having to visit a navy ship. I had not spent any quality time on a navy ship. I didn't do ships, and I was not an aircraft-carrier aviator. I had little to no sea time before being "haze gray and underway," as we say.

I was an NFO in a land-based, submarine-hunting P-3 Orion aircraft. I had seen a lot of navy ships in the open ocean from three hundred feet above at 250 knots.

My sea time was limited to a couple of weeks as a college midshipman on the USS *Nassau* (LHA-4) steaming in circles with a couple hundred embarked Marines off the coast of Beirut in 1984.

I also spent one week as a midshipman tied up in port in Norfolk, Virginia, on the USS *Merrimack* (AO-179)—an oiler—back in 1982.

On the *Merrimack*, the summer between my freshman and sophomore years, I slept a lot, painted things gray, had plenty of soft vanilla ice cream and cold chocolate milk in the galley, and swept the decks.

On the *Nassau*, underway in the Mediterranean Sea, the summer between my junior and senior years of college, I stood a lot of watches on the ship's bridge in the middle of the night. I decided I would rather stand watch on the bridge any time than be down in the sweltering, loud engine room. I also started my lifelong coffee addiction when a chief quartermaster handed me a cup of black coffee at 0345 on the bridge one morning when he saw me falling asleep standing up and said: "Here, drink this, Midshipman!"

Both ships are decommissioned now.

Navigating the bowels of a navy warship was hard for a P-3 NFO. There are gangways, bulkheads, berthing areas, galleys, passageways, a stern, a starboard, a port, a fo'c'sle, ladders, decks, "men working aloft," "sweepers manning brooms," a bow, a centerline, hatches, quarters, general quarters, pad eyes, cleats, an ensign flying, heads, an engine room, a quarterdeck, a bridge, an officers' wardroom, an enlisted galley, a chief's mess, a combat information center, and—if you were lucky—a flight deck!

When we had a shipboard meeting, I would usually request an escort because it was unlikely that I would have enough time to do proper advance work. The risk of failure was high.

As an NFO, I was a "brown shoe." When wearing my khaki uniform, I wore brown uniform shoes. The navy issued me a cool leather flight jacket.

The officers qualified to drive navy warships are surface warfare officers, or SWOs. We called them "black shoes" or just "shoes" for short. They wore black uniform shoes with their khaki uniform. They did not get a flight jacket.

There was then and still is a cultural difference in the navy between black shoes and brown shoes. The officers' wardroom for aviators was fun and congenial. We played jokes on one another and were always at the officers' club for happy hour by 1600 on Friday afternoon, after perhaps slipping away to play a round of golf first.

The black shoes didn't have nearly as much fun. For shoes, there was a major divide between junior officers and those who had made it to a department head tour on a ship. We used to say SWOs ate their young for breakfast after making them stand a twenty-four-hour watch.

A VISIT WITH THE BLACK SHOES

On one fine navy day, we were to visit a group of shoes on a small destroyer in Norfolk, Virginia. I had been on the job for a while at that point and felt pretty confident. I thought that I could navigate the small ship without an escort by using a diagram of the ship and some verbal directions.

"The wardroom is easy to find, Lieutenant Fava," the black-shoe executive officer of the ship assured me before the visit. I told the XO we would just meet him and the CO in the officers' wardroom, where they were gathered with the ship's crew of officers.

Perhaps a bit of complacency had set in. I discussed earlier how complacency is never good.

We flew in from Brunswick, arriving at the Norfolk Air Station on time. We had an official white navy vehicle waiting for us, which I drove over to the ship's pier. I pulled up to our reserved parking spot on the pier alongside the ship. I nodded to the spotter on the ship's quarterdeck as we hustled out of the car to board the ship.

As we walked up the gangway, the ship rendered the Admiral the appropriate military honors over the ship's loudspeaker, or 1MC. Four bells. Ding, ding . . . ding, ding. "Commander, Patrol Wings Atlantic arriving," accompanied by the high-pitched whistle of the bosun's pipe. We saluted the colors on the quarterdeck as we boarded the ship.

FIELD DAY AND POPEYE

Once on board, we were well on our way along the ship's passageways to the officers' wardroom when I rounded a corner and stopped. A large X of crisscrossed brown masking tape blocked our way. The tape was secured to the bulkheads on either side. It had a handwritten sign taped to it that read "SECURED for Field Day."

I glanced down the passageway and saw a Popeye-looking sailor in standard navy bell-bottom blue dungarees and a yellowing crew-neck T-shirt. He was laboring away with a buffer machine and a wax spray bottle. In the navy, a "field day" is an intense cleaning event. The dark, blue-tiled deck was beaming. It was slightly wet in some areas.

Popeye broke his buffer rhythm and gave me the eye as I gazed past the brown masking tape. He was not going to let us by. Nor was he interested in rendering the Admiral any greetings or honors.

He looked back down at the deck and continued his waxing. For this junior sailor, waxing the deck was slightly better than cleaning the heads or scraping paint.

ABOUT-FACE

Remain cool under pressure, I thought. We did an about-face. I started backtracking.

Following closely behind me, the Admiral muttered, "You know where you're going, Loop?"

"Yes, sir," I said.

I knew *where* we were going—to the officers' wardroom. What I did not know was how to get there.

I had two options.

I could try to navigate to the wardroom by directional guessing, or I could grab the first able-bodied person and ask for help. I looked at my watch. I had five minutes to get to the wardroom.

As luck would have it, a salty-looking navy chief was walking by. He had a rack of ribbons on his chest signifying some impressive military awards. I read his name tag. Option two it was!

"Good morning, Chief Johns. The Admiral is headed to the wardroom. Would you mind leading the way?" I said.

The Admiral continued to breathe down my neck, one half step behind me. Staring at the chief, I rolled my eyes back and up over my shoulder toward the Admiral.

"Aye, aye, sir! Follow me," the chief said. "Good morning, Admiral. Glad to have you on board, sir!"

Off we went down several passageways and around multiple corners.

As we entered each passageway, Chief Johns barked out, "Attention on deck!" That is the traditional navy announcement that a senior officer is coming forward into the space.

Hearing that, all the sailors would snap to attention. Those walking in the passageways pivoted sideways with their backs up against the bulkhead so we could proceed.

Chief Johns led us right to the wardroom hatch in under four minutes. He rapped on the door, pushed it open, stepped aside, and yelled, "Attention on deck!"

He then said, "Have a great day, Admiral."

"You too. Thank you, Chief," the Admiral said.

"Thank you, Chief," I said.

"Of course, 'L Tee'! Anything for the Admiral. Have a fine navy day!" And off he went.

We had arrived on time.

The chiefs are the backbone of the navy. As the senior enlisted personnel, they are the ones who get it done.

When my father commissioned me into the navy, he was a navy captain. He told me, "Son, you will do well if you always listen to your chiefs and take care of your sailors." This was one of the many times Dad was right.

WHAT I LEARNED

When you find yourself lost on the ship, in trouble, or in need of help, don't be afraid to ask for help in a timely fashion.

Years later, as an associate at a major law firm, when I missed a major filing deadline, potentially committing legal malpractice, I went to a senior partner several days after I realized my mistake. He told me the same. Always seek help quickly when you think you are in over your head. Problems do not get better with time. Acknowledge when you are in trouble. Swallow your pride and seek help early and often.

You will find that leaders and mentors will always lend a helping hand. And wise leaders also ask for help when they need it.

Chapter 10

DON'T PANIC UNDER PRESSURE

While serving as an aide, it was important that I remained calm when imminent failure seemed minutes away. No servicemember wants to be in the foxhole or on an aircraft with someone who panics or loses their cool.

SHIPMATES

Although a navy pilot, the Admiral was a sailor. He loved all aspects of the navy. He loved the sound of the ocean and the smell of saltwater. He was a salty admiral with bushy, unkempt gray eyebrows and a rough, dry, scaly face. His teeth were stained from years of black coffee. I inherited my love of the sea from my father, a navy captain, and from the Admiral. At heart, I am a sailor, too.

Many times, at the end of a long day, the Admiral would call a fellow naval officer or sailor "shipmate." That was his term to express camaraderie and appreciation. He called naval aviators shipmates, even though many considered themselves airedales, not shipmates. It was his term of endearment. As long as you had done a good job, he would shake your hand and say, "Thanks a lot, shipmate."

LET'S GO TO THE MARINA

When we traveled, we would build some free time into the schedule. We labeled "free time" as "admin" time. We published his schedule to the staff, so we did *not* want others to think the Admiral had a bunch of free time. Admin time sounded much better.

When on navy bases, the Admiral loved to drive by the marina and look at the sailboats because that's what sailors do. We love looking at sailboats and yachts and the ocean just as much as we love looking at aircraft carriers, frigates, destroyers, and cruisers.

One cool morning, we left Brunswick and flew into Norfolk Naval Air Station for an event the next day. It was a sweltering summer day in Norfolk when we arrived. We wore our khaki uniforms on the small navy C-12 transport aircraft.

Back then, the navy khaki uniform was made of a fabric known as certified navy twill, or CNT. It was 100 percent polyester and was supposed to hold a press better than 100 percent cotton. While it did do that, it was hot as hell. I might as well have been wearing a heavy-duty fifty-five-gallon trash bag. CNTs also trapped and retained moisture like a plastic bag. The navy later banned the uniform from shipboard wear because it could burn quickly, emit toxic smoke, and melt like plastic on your skin. I did *not* like that uniform.

I reserved an official white navy sedan for this trip. When we arrived, the ground crew drove the sedan up to the airplane as the aircraft's portside prop sputtered to a stop. The pilots kept the starboard engine running because we were a "drop-and-go" flight.

Before exiting the plane, the Admiral stuck his head into the cockpit.

"Thanks for the ride, shipmates," he said to the navy pilots, slapping them on the shoulders. We got off the aircraft after the aircrew lowered the door with its built-in ladder.

I got the Admiral and his luggage in the car. He jumped into the back seat. The admiral's one-star flag flew on a chrome yardarm attached to the front bumper. The headlights were on.

The flag flapped in the wind as we drove off. We'd driven several blocks when the Admiral said, "Hey Loop, pull over behind the gas station."

I knew the routine. I pulled over and turned off the headlights. I jumped out of the car and pulled the yardarm off the vehicle, rolled the flag up around the post, and tossed it in the back seat. The Admiral got out of the back seat and sat in the front passenger seat. Off we went.

He said, "Loop, we've got some time. Why don't we take a drive by the marina?"

"Sure thing, Admiral," I said.

I always planned ahead by knowing exactly where the marina was at any navy base we visited.

When we got to the marina, I drove along the gravel road that ran perpendicular to the docks. We had no specific purpose. No words were spoken. Just two sailors admiring the boats.

As we got to the end of the marina, I started to turn around by cutting the wheel hard to the left to make a U-turn in the front-wheel-drive car. The power steering groaned as the front wheels drove over the edge of the concrete boat trailer ramp that descended into the water. The ramp was elevated about five inches off the gravel in some places.

As we were gazing at the boats, a loud thud came from the car's right front. The car stopped. I heard the right front tire scratching and spinning. *Oh shit*, I thought. The car's undercarriage had landed on the boat ramp, leaving the right front wheel suspended in the air.

With the chassis stuck on the cement ramp, the car was going nowhere.

We didn't have a cell phone back then.

Although we were entitled to drive the car wherever he wanted on the navy base, technically the car was "For Official Use Only." A leisurely drive to the marina could be considered a "frolic and detour." This could be very embarrassing.

The Admiral rarely cussed. "Damn it, Mark, we're stuck." He grimaced.

We got out of the car. I surveyed the right front wheel. This was not good.

THE MARINE

I noticed a gentleman jogging by the marina in tight red nylon shorts and a yellow tank top emblazoned with *Semper Fi* in red letters.

He was right out of Central Casting for a US Marine.

Marine jogged up to us, dripping in sweat, put his hands on his hips, and said, "Sirs, looks like you gents might need a little assistance. Do you mind if I lend a hand?"

"That would be great, sir," I stated as the sweat beads grew on the top of my forehead. I suspect he was a senior enlisted Marine because he gave me an odd look due to my use of the word "sir."

Those who have served know that senior enlisted Marines don't take too kindly to being called "sir." I had made that mistake back in 1982 on the drill field in college when I said "Yes, sir" to Gunny Blendowski. "Don't call me sir, Midshipman Fava. I work for a living!"

At that time, responding "Yes, sir" was just an automatic response to someone who had just offered to help me as a result of my fine southern upbringing!

Marine stated, "Admiral, if you don't mind stepping aside, perhaps over that way"—he pointed—"we'll take care of this." The Admiral knew how to take direction when appropriate. He strolled away from the car.

Marine jogged over and retrieved a weathered four-by-four section of wood that was in the grass about forty feet from the car. He jammed it under the dangling right front tire. The water lapping at his fluorescent green running shoes did not distract him.

Marine said, "Get into the vehicle, sir, turn on the engine, and slowly put 'er in drive."

Marine remained in front of the car, just inches from the right front bumper, pushing the four-by-four under the tire as I started the car.

I eased on the accelerator as Marine crouched down at the bumper, nodding at me. I heard the tire begin to twist on the wood. He gave me a thumbs-up and waved his hand. I could barely see the top of his high and tight haircut. The car lurched forward, and the four-by-four creaked. I slammed on the brakes, making sure not to hit Marine. The right front tire dropped onto solid gravel, freeing the chassis from the ramp's edge.

Marine never flinched. He just stepped to the side in the water.

"Admiral, it looks like you are good to go, sir. Have a fine navy day," Marine said.

The Admiral looked at Marine, shook his hand, and said, "Thank you, Marine!" Although he could have, the Admiral knew not to call a Marine "shipmate."

"Yes, sir," he said. Mission complete, he took off across the grass and back to his running routine.

With the air conditioning on high cool in recirculation mode, I steered left to clear the water. I got out of the car to open the Admiral's door. He jumped into the front passenger seat.

As we drove away from the marina down the perimeter road, we headed toward Marine. He was sprinting on the shoulder of the black asphalt road in wet shoes and socks in the suffocatingly humid ninety-five-degree heat.

As we approached him from behind, he raised his left hand slightly. He didn't need to see us coming. He sensed our approach like any good Marine. He quickly shot a glance at me with a grin as we passed.

"That was not good," the Admiral stated as we drove toward our quarters, "but you can keep the job. Sometimes it's better to be lucky than good, Loop. And today, you got lucky, very lucky."

He laughed. I did not.

"Thank you, Admiral. Sorry about that," I said.

The car's air conditioning felt wonderful as the CNTs slowly lost the retained heat and the soaking moisture in the armpits of my white 100 percent cotton undershirt.

WHAT I LEARNED

When things go the wrong way, anxiety and stress kick in, potentially causing a loss of your temper. The ability to recognize the situation and remain calm will allow you to channel that anxiety into a successful outcome. No one likes a leader who rants and raves and uses profanity. Teams don't like teammates who lose their cool under pressure. I have done both. Neither is good.

The Admiral never lost his temper and never yelled at me. A leader should demonstrate that they can remain grounded under pressure and act logically when circumstances are not going as planned. Stay calm.

Chapter 11

BE CREATIVE WHEN THINGS DON'T GO AS PLANNED

Every minute of the day as an admiral's aide, I was thinking, *What are we doing now? What are we doing next? Where will we be in two, four, and six hours? What do I need to follow up on now for success tomorrow? Where will we be tomorrow?* I was always playing a what-if game.

Despite meticulous planning, the unexpected occurred. When that happened, I had to be innovative in creating an alternate plan for success.

Failure was not an option.

RENDERING HONORS AND MILITARY PROTOCOL

In the navy, military protocol and the proper rendering of honors are important.

Once when a three-star admiral aviator was coming to Brunswick, I saw some anxiousness that I typically did not see in the Admiral.

This was a big deal. Three stars are a dime a dozen in Washington, but not too many came to our sleepy base in Maine. The Admiral wanted to make sure everything went smoothly.

The Admiral asked, "Now Loop, you sure you have the three-star flags for the vehicle and the flagpole out front?"

"Yes, sir, I do," I said.

"And it's very important that his pennant only flies on the vehicle when the admiral's in the car," he stated.

"Of course, Admiral," I said. I knew that.

"And you have coordinated his arrival time with the base quarterdeck, so they know when he will be landing and when to strike his pennant at the headquarters?"

"Yes, sir," I repeated.

The three-star was coming to visit in the middle of winter. Having been raised in the South most of my life, I found Brunswick to be cold in the winter.

FREEZING RAIN, SNOW, AND ICE

Freezing rain fell throughout the night before the three-star flew in. Meteorologists predicted the temperatures would drop further the next morning due to an approaching low-pressure system.

Knowing the three-star's flight was to arrive at zero seven thirty, I was awake at "zero dark thirty" in the morning. The sidewalk outside my two-bedroom townhouse was covered in a sheet of ice and frozen snow. Icicles hung from the roof over my front door. When I backed my car out of my garage, the pine tree branches hung low and sparkled with ice. I could hear the frozen ground pop and crackle under my tires.

I carefully drove to the base to get the official navy vehicle warmed up. I would park my own car and drive the official vehicle with the Admiral and the visiting three-star as passengers.

I had parked the navy sedan outside on the navy base. It was a white, boxy, four-door Chrysler K-car with a blue fake leather interior. It had a large, clunky first-generation Motorola cellular phone mounted on the center console.

Ruffled ice covered the K-car. The doors were frozen shut. After knocking the ice off the driver's door, I got inside and turned the ignition. The car struggled to start. It eventually turned over with a roar and a plume of white exhaust.

I turned the heater and defrosters on high. Then I climbed back out to clear the snow and ice with a plastic scraper. Even with my gloves on, my hands quickly became red and stiff from the cold.

I had parked the fully fueled car near the arrival location of the vice admiral's plane. I also had the three-star pennant for the vehicle in my briefcase. After clearing most of the snow and ice off the front windshield, I planned on sitting in the car for at least an hour to warm it up.

As the air inside warmed, the ice remnants slid off the windows. I retrieved the three-star flag attached to the silver chrome rod and got out of the car. Carefully, I began making my way to the front of the vehicle on the ice-covered pavement so I could insert the chrome pole into the yardarm post attached to the car's front bumper.

It was a simple contraption. Just a flag on a metal rod that slid down into a hollow metal post with a small screw at the bottom of the post to lock the rod in place.

It was still dark, with a freezing drizzle coming down. When I got to the front bumper, the pole would not slide into the hole in the mast arm. I had preflighted the yardarm mast the day before, and the flagpole rod had slid easily into the mast.

I tried to jam it in a couple more times without success. *Whiskey Tango Foxtrot? Had the metal contracted in the cold overnight?*

Then it dawned on me. Overnight, the hollow metal yardarm mast had filled up with freezing rain. The freezing rain had turned into solid ice. I tried to bend the rod back and forth to crack the ice. Nothing. Frozen solid. Stiff as could be.

Dammit, I thought. *This is not good!* I looked at my watch.

I needed a heat source to warm the rod. If I only had a cigarette lighter, perhaps I could heat the rod.

I immediately opened up my "brain," which I always carried with me, to my page of base phone numbers. I located the phone number of the twenty-four-hour hotline for the base's Public Works Department. The Public Works Department was the facilities group that handled maintenance on all the military buildings and vehicles. They had a hotline for on-base maintenance emergencies. This was an emergency. I used the clunky car cell phone and dialed the hotline.

"NAS Brunswick Public Works, Petty Officer Campos. How may I help you, sir or ma'am?" the voice said.

I did not hesitate to use the Admiral's stars.

"Good morning, Petty Officer Campos. This is Lieutenant Fava. I am the aide to the Admiral. The Admiral needs a handheld blow torch. I assume you have one there and are qualified to use it?" I asked.

"We do, sir. When does the Admiral need it?" he said.

"Right now. I'm on my way to your building. I'll be there in five minutes. Please meet me outside at the official navy white vehicle with the blowtorch lit and ready to go."

I'm sure the young sailor thought I was crazy, but he simply stated, "Sir, yes, sir. I'll see you here shortly."

I glanced at my watch again. I had fifteen minutes before I had to meet the Admiral with the vehicle. When I pulled up to the Public Works building, Petty Officer Campos was outside the door in his black peacoat and white Dixie Cup cover, standing with a lit handheld blowtorch.

I explained that we needed to heat the mast arm carefully. Without hesitation, Campos began sweeping the blowtorch up and down the mast yardarm a few inches away so as not to char the silver enamel. In a matter of seconds, the mast arm started to sizzle from the top until water was boiling out of the yardarm.

I jammed the rod with the unfurled three-star pennant into the yardarm. I tightened the base screw to hold the mast in place.

I thanked Petty Officer Campos and shook his hand. I drove off, arriving back at the rendezvous point to meet the Admiral within minutes of his showing up.

We greeted the vice admiral upon arrival. I unfurled the three-star pennant when we pulled up to his aircraft. He had come without his aide. I had reassured his loop, whose aiguillette had three gold-and-dark-blue spiral loops, as opposed to my two loops, that I would take care of his boss. And I did.

SUCCESS

The rest of the day went off without a hitch. All the visit's details fell into place nicely.

"Great job today, Loop," the Admiral stated at the end of the twelve-hour day. "The vice told me you were one of the best loops he has ever worked with. And he works with a lot of them! Thank you."

It was late in the afternoon and getting dark when the three-star left.

"You've worked half a day today, so take the rest of the day off, shipmate," the Admiral said to me with a loud chuckle and a backslap.

"Thank you, Admiral. See you tomorrow!"

Good days were great days! They were long, but satisfying when I avoided failure.

I went back to my townhouse and took a hot shower. I was lonely and missed home. *Maybe I should have married her already*, I thought.

I pulled out the next day's schedule and reviewed it. I fell asleep on the sofa in front of the TV as it started to snow.

Of course, Petty Officer Campos got a personal thank-you note on the Admiral's letterhead the following week. I told the Admiral why we needed to send him one, and he laughed. He said, "That's why I hired you, Loop!"

I drafted the letter to Campos. It went something like this:

Dear Petty Officer Campos,

Thank you very much for your recent assistance in helping prepare the official navy vehicle for the arrival of Vice Admiral Faulkner. Your flexibility and expertise allowed for the start of an exceptionally important visit to me.

You are the epitome of the "can-do" sailor who makes the United States Navy the best navy in the world. Thank you again for a job exceptionally well done, shipmate!

Respectfully,
The Admiral

WHAT I LEARNED

I was always thinking ahead. This planning mindset served me very well as I matured into a senior naval officer and in my careers as a lawyer and corporate executive. A leader needs to have a what-if future mindset.

Be creative, especially when things do not go as planned. When the original plan failed, flexibility, creativity, and innovation saved me more than once.

I am sure I could have just told the Admiral that the mast yardarm was frozen and there was nothing we could do, but thinking outside the box for a solution was what I was paid to do.

Years later, in my senior executive corporate legal job, I had made a bad decision and was getting a real verbal scrubbing by the general counsel on the phone. He reminded me again of the importance of always thinking ahead. I had provided some advice that the boss did not think was good, and I hadn't anticipated what had happened as a result.

He stated to me, "Mark, people who make those kinds of decisions get fired where I come from!"

After being in the receiving mode for a few minutes, I blurted out, "I'm sorry. I just didn't see that issue coming."

He responded, "Don't ever use that excuse with me again, Fava. I pay you to see things coming. That's why you are there."

Don't let the roadblocks get in the way. Think ahead. Expect the unexpected. Find a way, and carry on with a plan!

Chapter 12

BE A TEAM PLAYER

As an aide, I was successful not only because I worked hard, but also because I was a member of a close-knit team. We were aligned with a mission. Our goal was to make the Admiral successful in executing his vision and direction. I relied on that team, and I was a team player.

THE ADMIRAL'S TEAM

The Admiral's staff consisted of about ten other officers, all significantly senior in rank to me. His front office consisted of me, the chief of staff (a navy captain), the flag secretary (a navy lieutenant commander), and the Admiral's flag writer (a navy senior chief). The chief of staff and the flag sec also wore loops.

We were a great team. Here's why.

Captain Bruce Jansen was the chief of staff, or COS. He wore silver eagles on his collar. He ran the staff as the Admiral's senior confidant. COS was a big, bald, burly man with a large head and a round stomach that hung slightly over his uniform waistline. He usually had a pipe in his mouth. It was rarely lit unless it was after hours and he was standing near his cracked-open office window.

Captain Jansen had neat stacks of papers and manila folders adorned with yellow stickies and black clips rising four to five inches high across his desk. Despite the appearance of chaos, he knew where everything was. And he had a great sense of humor.

He called me Bud, as in the following:

"Bud, look here. Why don't you step into my office, and let's see if we can unscrew this mess before it gets to the Admiral."

"Bud, boss ain't gonna like this turd. It has the makings of a real shitshow, so let's discuss it and the best time and way for me to raise it with the boss."

"Bud, take these written award citations with you on your trip tomorrow to Iceland so the Admiral can present them there. Make sure you don't forget them. That wouldn't be good. In fact, that would royally suck for you."

And my favorite, with his pipe in hand, late on a Friday afternoon when we were the only two left in the building:

"Bud, it's late, and we're soon to be the only motivated bastards in this damn building other than the front door sentry. This mess will be here Monday. I say we secure and head over to the O club for a cold beer."

Like the Admiral, he was full of wisdom and a pilot also. He knew that he would never promote to flag rank. His purpose was to support the Admiral and run the staff—and he was very good at it.

The flag writer was Senior Chief Rebecca Mooney. She also managed the Admiral's schedule, helped with our travel packets, and choreographed the daily meetings and phone calls. She prepared all the Admiral's correspondence, including the thank-you notes. She was what we call today an executive office assistant—and a really good one. Most importantly, she was a navy senior chief.

She'd been working for the Admiral long before I arrived, so she knew him better than I did. Quite frankly, she saved my ass on several occasions. She guided me by saying, "I don't think you should do that, Lieutenant" or "The Admiral won't like that, Lieutenant." And she was always right.

I could call her anytime with a logistical issue or a scheduling problem from anywhere in the world. She would always answer the phone and reassure me: "Don't worry about it, Lieutenant. I got it." She held down the front office when we were on the road.

Senior didn't wear a loop, but she didn't need to. Everyone knew who she was in the headquarters building and on the base. She, too, could use the Admiral's stars when needed.

The flag secretary was another senior P-3 pilot on his shore duty tour. He would later become the commanding officer of a P-3 squadron after leaving the staff (something I did fourteen years later). He also took care of me.

The COS, the flag writer, the flag sec, and I worked flawlessly together as a team. We were all aligned in our purpose. We were a hardworking and fun group.

The staff was rounded out with officer department heads and very sharp enlisted sailors from the most junior petty officer to a command master chief, the most senior enlisted rank in the navy. The department heads included an operations officer, a public affairs officer, a flight surgeon, and my favorite, a JAG lawyer. As a young lieutenant with only about five years in the navy, I was usually the most junior officer in the room—or the building, for that matter.

As a loop, I wielded a lot of power. Many officers who outranked me did what I said without question. Being a team player was important. I had to gain the trust of the Admiral's front office and the entire staff.

My reputation depended on how well I took care of the Admiral and how well I worked with the staff.

POINT TO THE ASSIST

I implemented a couple of practices as a team player.

First, I always gave credit when credit was due. For example, the Admiral was frequently a guest speaker at military and civilian events. I worked with his staff and the public affairs officer (PAO) in preparing and polishing his remarks. The PAO wrote the first draft of many speeches, but I had complete license to edit the script based on what I knew about the Admiral or the event's details.

I edited his speeches based on information I gathered from advance phone calls with the event's coordinator. Making the speech personal resulted in it being impactful and connected the Admiral with his audience. My goal was for the audience to recognize every speech as exceptional.

When someone complimented the Admiral about his speech, he would say, "Well, you can thank the loop; he wrote it for me. I saw it for the first time yesterday morning."

I would then say, "Well, you should really thank the PAO for this one!"

Just as the Admiral had done, I would redirect the praise to another member of our team. When the news of such credit got back to the PAO, he appreciated it.

GIVE OTHERS A HEADS-UP

Also, as a loop, I was a team player by giving other officers on the staff insight or a heads-up when it was appropriate to do so. For example, if I were in a meeting with the Admiral and he asked me to have one of his staff officers come see him on an issue, I would tell the staff member what the subject matter was in advance of their meeting with the Admiral.

There was nothing wrong with doing that. It provided for efficiency of process and adequate preparation of the staff officers in their interaction with the Admiral. Those answering his beckoning call did not have to say, "I'm not sure, Admiral. I will have to get back to you on that." Knowing the subject matter in advance, they arrived prepared with a plan to address the Admiral's concerns.

The Admiral would appreciate it because the officer came prepared. A little heads-up to others was a great way to be a team player. The staff appreciated this also. No one wanted to be called on the carpet or caught unprepared in front of the Admiral.

COVER FOR OTHERS

Finally, being a team player meant that I covered for others. To do this, I got to know others both professionally and personally. I had some awareness of the staff's personal lives.

For example, when I knew that the operations officer had an event to attend at his daughter's elementary school one morning, I covered for him. I ensured that no one scheduled a meeting involving him during that time frame. If someone was looking for him, I told them, "He is unavailable, but I'd be happy to help you with any issue you might have and pass that along to him."

I'm not saying I'd cover up for people as in lie, mislead, or hide the facts. If the Admiral asked, "Where is the Ops O?" I would say, "Sir, he's got a personal family matter that he is handling this morning, and I told him I would cover for him." The Admiral appreciated that.

Later, I would inform the operations officer, "Sir, while you were out, the Admiral was looking for you. I think it was about next week's staff meeting, if you can get back to him ASAP."

WHAT I LEARNED

In summary, being a team player is easy. Do it!

Wherever you work, be a team player. In large part, your reputation and success will be based on whether others see you as part of the team or a jerk, a one-way "blocking diode." Team players win for themselves and others. One-ways succeed for a while, but their lack of a loyal following will limit their success in the end. And no one will be there to help them if they falter.

Fast forward many years later to corporate meetings, when another colleague singled me out for assisting with a successful external event. I made a point of deflecting the praise, stating, "Well, you know, it was the government operations director who was responsible for this event and made it such a success for us."

Then at a meeting later in the week, when someone singled out the government ops director, she stated, "Indeed, it was just a great day for us, but it was really Mark's work that made it such a successful event."

I once worked with another gentleman who was not a team player. While the successful execution of both of our functions depended on us working well together and sharing information, he did not do so. In fact, it appeared to me that he purposefully hid information from me, treating our professional relationship like some kind of competition. Dysfunction and surprises were the result. Both of our jobs became frustrating. It was a chore interacting with him. After a year, it had become obvious to many, especially his boss, who asked others how things were going. His boss removed him from that job.

As people are promoted, some forget the importance of being a team player. That can be detrimental to the group's morale and one's reputation. As your career progresses, it's a small world. You will likely encounter many of the same colleagues in the future. They will remember whether you were a team player.

More bluntly stated, the general counsel and my boss at the time once told me, "You are of no value to me if they don't like you and they don't invite you to the meetings."

Bosses like to promote team players. Team players get invited to the meetings and become team leaders.

Chapter 13

BE DEPENDABLE

I learned during my time in Brunswick that reliability and dependability mattered. When I made a commitment, I had to keep it.

The loop community was very close. We could depend on one another.

Unlike every other request I made, which I checked and double-checked, I rarely needed to follow up on a commitment from another loop. If you wore a loop, other aides automatically granted you the "speed of trust" as a member of the close circle. We knew the why of getting the job done. More importantly, we knew the significant risk and potential outcome of failure.

BEAUTIFUL BRUNSWICK

Although demanding, being the aide to the only admiral in Brunswick, Maine, was a great job. Brunswick was a quaint New England town.

Unlike other industrial-looking navy bases, the only function at the Brunswick Naval Base was naval aviation. There were no big gray ships.

The town had a Maine Street (not a typo) and an adjacent park with a white gazebo and a nice strip of green space. Maine Street was lined with small restaurants and shops.

The nearby areas of Bath, Bailey Island, Harpswell, and Orr's Island were perfect for a summer drive to enjoy a lobster dinner and a cold beer, or a fall cabin stay on the rocky shoreline with a wood stove warming the room.

Brunswick had a small-town feel. Fat Boy Drive-In sat right outside the base fence at the end of the runway. It was right out of the 1950s. Built in 1955, the restaurant still retained its classic feel. You could get fried clam baskets, hamburgers, lobster rolls, onion rings, and french fries. Then top it off with a vanilla or orange cream frappe. Car service was part of the experience. All you needed to do was pull up to a spot and turn your lights on when you were ready for the carhop.

Brunswick has changed a lot since 1990, but not Fat Boy Drive-In, which thankfully seems to be stuck in the 1950s. It's still there serving great frappes. I rode through there with my family in the summer of 2022 on vacation as we drove up the coast from the Cape to Maine. What was once a vibrant Cold War P-3 naval air station is now a hodgepodge of odd businesses that appear to have been shoehorned into the buildings once used by the navy. Gone is the house where the Admiral lived, replaced by some new three-story apartments. The baseball fields, once full of sailors playing summer softball, are overgrown, with nothing but the chain-link backstops still visible.

HELP WITH TRIP PLANNING

Because Brunswick was so nice in the summer, we received our fair share of visitors. Many of the Admiral's personal friends and other flag officers came to the area on military leave with their families. When that occurred, the aide of the other flag officer would call me, asking logistical questions about lodging, restaurants, and other attractions.

Of course, as part of the loop network, I was happy to assist fellow loops in answering any questions they had. Others loops knew they could depend on my help and advice just like I could depend on them.

SO MANY LOBSTERS

In addition to being a wonderful place to live, Brunswick was the best place in the navy to buy as many lobsters as you wanted. Much like the many shrimp dishes in the movie *Forrest Gump*, Maine had all kinds of delicious lobster dishes. There were lobster rolls, small lobsters, big lobsters, culls, lobster casserole, lobster salad, baked lobster, lobster stew, lobster mac 'n' cheese (my favorite!), lobster salad, lobster ravioli, and of course, warm bowls of creamy "lobstah chowdah."

I arranged for the deliveries of hundreds of pounds of lobster to navy colleagues and friends around the world. These lobsters were shipped live to be cooked and served with melted butter at large social events and small family dinners hosted by admirals and military friends.

As a northeast coastal air station, Brunswick had a constant throughput of all kinds of military aircraft. Many would be coming from or headed to overseas destinations. They would land for a quick gas-and-go stop before continuing to their destination.

Occasionally, orange-edged navy training jets would drop in during their cross-country flights with a lieutenant flight instructor and a young ensign student naval aviator. They would typically arrive on a Friday afternoon for a weekend stay. Before departure, they would find some compartment in the jet just large enough to store a small box of lobsters to take home to their spouses.

I could get any quantity of live lobsters to any destination in the world as long as there was an existing flight headed in the right direction.

J&A SEAFOOD MARKET

My predecessor, Lieutenant Samuel Jackson, told me during my turnover, "For all lobster requests, just call Mike at J&A Seafood."

Lobster requests—what the hell? I thought.

Sam had briefed me thoroughly over our couple-of-weeks' turnover. It was like drinking from a firehose. As you recall, he also told me about carrying wooden toothpicks.

J&A Seafood Market was a relatively small, red, barnlike building with a white-trimmed door. The smell of fish and the sound of bubbling water from huge wooden and metal lobster tanks hit you when you walked in. The gray cement floor behind the wood counter was always wet.

The lobster requests came in regularly from loops around the country.

I remember one request in the early winter for more than one hundred medium-sized lobsters to be delivered to Naval Air Station Roosevelt Roads in Puerto Rico.

"Hey, Lieutenant Fava, this is Lieutenant Burton, the aide for the commander of Southern Command in Puerto Rico. In about two weeks, my admiral is having a dinner party at his quarters for some VIPs. I heard you could assist me in getting some live lobsters," the aide said.

"Sure, that's me. How many do you need and exactly when?" I asked with pen in hand and paper ready to go. Most days in the office, there was not a lot of time for bullshit when the Admiral was there. Just get right to the point, please.

The aide continued. "He's having about one hundred guests, so we're looking for about one hundred and ten lobsters, one to two pounds each. We need them that Friday afternoon around 1600 so they can be cooked at the party. We heard a P-3 from Brunswick is coming down to Puerto Rico that day."

"Got it. One hundred ten, one to two pounds." I repeated the order like any good NFO communicator. "Not a problem at all. I've got it on my calendar. Let's touch base a few days before to confirm an existing flight and the logistics."

I made one call to Mike at J&A with the orders. The rest worked like clockwork. J&A never failed me! They packed the lobsters in cardboard boxes or white Styrofoam coolers filled with ice. They wrapped them in newspaper with their claws bound by thick yellow bands, sealed the boxes with brown masking tape, and attached a handwritten receipt to the box.

J&A would deliver the boxes to the aircraft on the flight-line tarmac minutes before engine start. They had complete access to any of the locked airfield perimeter fence gates by calling the squadron duty office and stating which aircraft they were going to.

I made sure the squadron duty officer and aircrew were aware of the importance of these packages. I used the Admiral's stars to get their attention by stating, "The delivery of these packages is very important to the Admiral."

During the week of this order, the weather forecaster predicted a significant nor'easter coming through Maine later in the week. Late Thursday night, blizzard conditions set in, dumping nearly a foot of fresh snow.

As the snowfall continued, I worried that the lobsters were not going to make it to Puerto Rico the next day, either because the squadron was going to cancel the flight due to the snow or that the roads might become impassable for J&A's truck to make it to the base.

I called J&A around 0400 Friday morning because the departing flight was taking off approximately three hours later. The phone rang. No one answered.

I called the squadron duty office and told them to call me when J&A showed up. I reminded them that I expected the truck to come through the flight-line gate between 0630 and 0645, before the 0700 departure, with several packages.

I called J&A's landline again. No answer.

Around 0645, my home phone rang as I was preparing to go to the office. "Lieutenant Fava, this is Lieutenant JG Shepard in the VP–26 duty office. The J&A guy just loaded the packages on the aircraft. The aircraft has been preflighted, and the runways are clear. Trident 158 is scheduled for an on-time departure of 0700."

I was late getting to the headquarters' office, around 0715, but trucks had salted and cleared the roads. More than a foot of snow had been covering them.

In Maine, clearing snow off the roads was routine. Huge yellow dump trucks with flashing yellow lights and plows attached to their front bumpers blasted down the major roads at over forty miles per hour, throwing snow twenty to thirty feet in the air to the road's shoulder.

The locals in their pickup trucks helped clear the outlying roads with their yellow detachable plows mounted on their front bumpers. During the summer, those plows would sit in the side yard rusting a little more each year and surrounded by weeds and wildflowers.

As soon as I got to my desk, the phone rang.

"Maaackk, this is Mike. I gotcha lobstah over to VP-26 on time. It was a little hairy this morning, but you know me. If we say we're gonna do it, we're gonna do it. I saw the weather forecast last night and packed the lobstah up in extra ice to get them really cold, and I took them home. They stayed overnight in my garage. They'll be fine—good and cold. I got up at five to make sure I could get to the plane in time."

"Mike, you are incredible," I told him. "I owe you one."

"You owe me nuttin', my friend. Just keep those orders a-comin'. And I threw in a couple extra lobstah because you're such a good customer."

About a week later, I received a check made out to J&A Seafood Market, wrapped in a short note and stuffed into an envelope. The aide wrote the check out for the exact amount that had been on the handwritten invoice taped to the boxes. I hand-delivered the check to J&A on my way home.

I received a personal thank-you letter from the lobster-receiving flag officer. I knew the aide had written the note. We took care of each other. Such notes on the Admiral's stationery were a nice touch. I filed them in a manila folder in my desk drawer labeled "atta-boys."

The note said something like this:

> *Dear Lieutenant Fava,*
> *I wanted to personally thank you for your recent help with one of our major command functions. Your reliability, dependability, and attention to detail were clearly displayed in how you responded to our request for assistance. The event could not have been such a success without your contribution. Thank you for a job well done!*
>
> *Regards,*
> *Admiral Jefferies*

WHAT I LEARNED

I arranged for the delivery of hundreds of pounds of lobsters during my time as an aide. J&A taught me the importance of credibility, reliability, and dependability, and how it was essential to follow through with a commitment, even in extreme circumstances, because people depended on you and your word.

Your reputation over time depends on how well you keep your commitments. Senior leaders value a trustworthy employee. Leaders are dependable.

Chapter 14

LOYALTY AND INTEGRITY

It was my job to make the Admiral look good. I protected him and steered him away from trouble.

A career as a navy officer is pretty rewarding, yet it can be an unforgiving profession. With the responsibility and authority of a senior officer comes accountability. If a ship runs aground or collides with another ship at sea, even if the captain is not on the deck with the con (driving the ship), they are responsible for that incident. At times, senior leadership relieves the commanding officer before the navy completes its investigation. Also, officers are expected to act with integrity and not break the law.

With the leadership and authority vested in the Admiral came the responsibility to make difficult decisions, the outcomes of which did not please everyone. When a tough issue landed on the Admiral's desk, many other intelligent people had been unable to address it. They might not have had the authority to do so, or on the other hand, perhaps they lacked the wisdom to choose the best path forward, so they punted it up the chain of command to the Admiral.

The Admiral was in a position of command and authority. Those in command make tough choices and issue orders to carry them out. They could involve life-and-death decisions in which the Admiral was placing young warfighters in harm's way.

Admirals also make more routine choices, such as sending a detachment out of the country over the Christmas holiday or extending a carrier battle group's deployment for several months after an arduous six-month deployment. Admirals can cancel periods of planned leave due to emergent situations or an international crisis. They can send sailors and Marines at a moment's notice around the world, requiring them to miss birthdays, the births of their children, anniversaries, and the deaths of their parents. That's part of their job and that of any leader—making the tough decisions and being responsible and accountable for the outcomes.

It was my job to be loyal and support the Admiral's decisions.

INTEGRITY AS A LOOP

I learned about accountability and integrity as a loop. I was the Admiral's second conscience, steering him away from any potential trouble. No one else could tell him no as easily as I could. If it didn't look right, sound right, smell right, or was just outright not right, I told the Admiral, "Not a good idea, sir."

With those stars came a lot of new visibility and extra scrutiny. People were always watching the boss.

While flag officers are smart, the stars can go to their heads, and the fanfare can become intoxicating. Every year, some flag officers make the front pages of *Navy Times*, ending an otherwise fabulous career because of a dumb mistake or unintentional misstep.

I was fortunate. The Admiral had integrity and was well respected. I took care of him, and in turn, he took care of me.

HURRY UP AND WAIT—WITH OTHER LOOPS

As an admiral's aide, I spent hours with other loops in hallways or holding rooms, "milling about smartly." There we would wait for our bosses, who were in meetings or attending flag conferences. During those times, after we had confirmed every detail of the next event on the schedule, we would chat about our experiences, laugh at our circumstances, and share in our misery. We would swap sea stories about our successes and failures.

We would also hear scuttlebutt about the latest loop to be fired or admiral to be relieved of command. We would share stories about "not-so-smart" things the Admiral wanted to do. I got to know a lot of other aides during those times. As I have discussed, we had a strong network—we walked in the same shoes.

LOYALTY AS A LOOP

As a loop, my only boss and priority was the Admiral. Unwavering loyalty was critical.

It was my job to be loyal and support his decisions.

While I was to support the Admiral, he allowed me to take "leave and liberty" to disagree with him behind closed doors. I did this diplomatically. He might ask me what I thought, or I "requested permission to speak freely." Loyalty demanded that I tell the truth. It's easy to fall into the "emperor with no clothes" scenario and parrot back to a boss what you think they want to hear. The harder position is to provide honest advice that the boss might not want to hear. That's what I did as an aide.

Once I had spoken my mind and the Admiral made a decision and issued an order, I walked out of his office and supported the decision unequivocally. That was loyalty.

When others told me that they thought the Admiral's decision was misguided, I did not engage in debate.

"Mark, what in the world is he thinking?" a senior staff officer once said. "I mean, we can do this, but it just doesn't make any sense at all."

I responded, "Well, sir, you surely are entitled to your opinion, but the Admiral has made his decision, and it's time to execute. You can speak with him if you have any questions, but he's not changing his mind." Once everyone knew where I stood as far as my loyalty to the Admiral, I rarely heard additional complaints.

TAKING CARE OF THE BOSS

The Admiral did not need much babysitting. Some of my colleagues were not so fortunate.

He was early to bed and early to rise. He was the life of a social event and a charming man, but not one to stay until the end of a party or drink heavily.

"Make sure I am up on time tomorrow," the Admiral would say at the end of a long day in Jacksonville.

"Aye, aye, Admiral," I would say. "Good night, sir."

The next morning, at 0630, he might be running a few minutes late. I would gently rap on his room door.

"How do I look?" he would ask when he opened the door in his dress choker white uniform. We were headed to a squadron change-of-command ceremony where he was the guest speaker. I inspected his uniform from head to toe. He had bloodshot eyes.

"Wings are a little crooked, sir. And let's get a hit of the Visine. Barn door is slightly open. Otherwise excellent, Admiral." I would level his Wings of Gold on his uniform and hand him the bottle of Visine that I kept in my briefcase. I grabbed his white gloves, military sword, cover, and speech binder. Off we would go.

WHAT I LEARNED

Loyalty is important. As an aide, I knew loyalty was something the Admiral deserved, demanded, and expected. That included my disagreeing behind closed doors and supporting his decisions everywhere else. It also meant making sure he was always seen in the best light. I have used these practices in my civilian jobs as both a follower and a leader over the years.

That's how loyalty and leadership should work. If you take care of your people, you'll find they will work hard for you, protect your six, and cover for you. They work hard because they like you and they want to, not because they have to. Most importantly, your team will achieve incredible results. Be loyal. Keep your boss and other colleagues out of and away from trouble. Speak up and say what is on your mind.

As a young lawyer at a big law firm, a wise partner once reminded me that we were not being paid to tell the client what they wanted to hear (there were many others who would do that, he said), but rather to provide sound legal advice, which sometimes means telling clients things they don't want to hear.

If you get to the point in your job when you are questioning your loyalty to your employer, it might be time to move on. I have done that in my career. Until then, being loyal is a sign of a trusted partner and a leader.

As far as integrity and doing the right thing, I am reminded of a sign at the flight school gate in Pensacola, Florida, that stated, "If there's doubt, there's no doubt." I did not truly understand that as a junior officer, but the older I got and during my time as an aide, the more that made sense. It still does today.

Finally, integrity always trumps loyalty. Always do the right thing and steer clear of trouble. One dumb decision can end any chance you have of becoming a leader.

Chapter 15

SENIORITY MATTERS

The concept is simple yet important because situational awareness of seniority matters. Regarding seniority, I am not speaking of age or tenure, but rather positional seniority, as to where you are on the org chart compared to others.

In the navy, every officer has a lineal number. The lineal number defines exactly where you stand in terms of seniority to all other commissioned officers. You can compare your number to any other officer's lineal number—including those with your same rank—and determine whether you are junior or senior to the other officer.

As a loop, the admiral's seniority with respect to other admirals was important. I needed to know this to choreograph his day correctly. I used my knowledge of seniority to arrange telephone calls with other admirals, determine seating arrangements at official functions, and ensure the proper rendering of military honors.

PICK UP THE PHONE

For example, I needed to know seniority in coordinating the Admiral's phone calls with other flag officers.

When the Admiral asked me to connect him with another one-star admiral, I would look up the other admiral in the "admiral's seniority book." That book listed from top to bottom the most senior admirals in the navy—from the chief of naval operations, or CNO—to the most junior admiral. I could figure out exactly where my admiral stood in relation to every other navy flag officer.

Telephone etiquette was essential. The junior admiral always got on the phone first and waited for the senior admiral. I might stay on the line to listen to the conversation. It was common in routine matters for many loops to remain on the line, take notes, and be prepared to help with the postcall action items, always recognizing that confidentiality mattered and absolutely nothing in that telephone conversation left the room.

I screwed up the order once and had the senior admiral join the call and hold for my boss. I heard the Admiral apologize as soon as he joined the call. After the conversation, he came out of his office and said, "Mark, you did know that Admiral Hearne was senior to me? That was very awkward for me. No big deal, but don't let that happen again," he said.

"Yes, sir."

WHERE'S MY SEAT?

For meetings, I knew all the attendees, their positions, and their seniority. I verified there had been no late add-ons or cancellations leading up to the meeting. Before we arrived, I briefed the Admiral.

I also knew the seating arrangement and confirmed where he would sit.

Seniority mattered with respect to seating at military functions. Seating precedence always depended on rank and seniority. This would be the case at change-of-command ceremonies and formal military dinners. Flawlessly coordinating the seating arrangement for a military function was hard when it involved many attendees. However, getting this right was simply part of the "attention to detail" required for being a loop.

Seniority also mattered concerning arrival times. As I have already discussed, if the junior admiral were to meet the senior admiral at a specific building or location, his aide made sure he got there first, never keeping the senior admiral waiting.

The flag officers usually did not need to look at the seniority book. They knew very well who was above and below them in terms of seniority.

WHAT I LEARNED

In the civilian professional world, many individuals need help understanding their place in an organizational chart in relation to others. While a person might look five to ten years younger than you, that person might be very senior to you in terms of their position. You need to know that. And you need to be aware of that before you engage with others in person or by email.

As a corporate lawyer, I've made the mistake of being too aggressive or naïve with respect to the individual contacting me about an issue, only to find out that person was much senior to me.

On the other hand, I have had very junior employees send me an abrupt email with a red exclamation point demanding that I complete some trivial task ASAP! That person lacks situational awareness.

Situational awareness is essential for workplace success. At all meetings, you should know the agenda and the attendees' titles, especially if you are pitching at the meeting. You also need to know who the decision-maker is. You are behind the power curve if you walk into any discussion without knowing who's who in the zoo.

Do your homework. Knowing who the senior players are demonstrates you have a level of situational awareness that is a sign of a leader.

Chapter 16

FAMILY TRIPS

As I have stated, one of the many rules as an aide was that I was never to embarrass the Admiral. If I needed to get adversarial with someone, I did not do so in the Admiral's presence.

I also learned that I should not lose my temper. That rule was then—and is still—a challenging one for me, especially when things are not going as planned. In fact, a leadership coach told me that I can be impatient and excitable at times.

I made many trips with the Admiral as his sole traveling companion. There were also some trips when I was included with the Admiral's family.

When his family traveled with him for an official event, I ensured we complied with the navy's ethical rules requiring the Admiral to pay for his family's expenses. Sometimes the trip would be just with the Admiral and his gracious wife, Janie. He called her his "number-one shipmate." On other occasions, the trips included his entire family with his two grown children.

On family trips, the Admiral was incredibly kind. He started the journey by saying, “Mark, we’re glad you could come with us. Consider yourself part of the family.”

I really did not have a choice as to whether I was going on the family trip if official duties were involved, but I appreciated the kind words. Whenever I was with him, it was work. I was on duty. I was not really part of the family on these trips.

DOOR COUNTY, WISCONSIN

One of my most memorable “all in the family” trips was to beautiful Sturgeon Bay, Wisconsin, in August 1990. Sturgeon Bay is located in Door County, in the middle of the seventy-mile-long peninsula that reaches well into Lake Michigan on the eastern side of Wisconsin.

We were headed there because the Admiral’s wife, Janie, had been chosen to christen a new navy minesweeper built by Peterson Building Inc. (PBI). PBI was an incredible American success story as a family-owned, multigenerational ship-building company.

Although it has since closed, at the height of its business, PBI had over one thousand employees and constructed more than eight hundred ships for thirteen countries. In the early nineties, it was known for its expertise in building beautiful wooden-hull minesweepers with minimal metal to maximize their countermine capabilities. A large metallic object would trigger a mine, so a wooden hull was ideal for a minesweeper.

The Sturgeon Bay trip included the whole family—the Admiral, Janie, their son, JD, and their daughter, Sandy, along with her husband.

Door County in August was much like Maine. Crisp and chilly at night, with cool weather and clear blue skies during the day.

GREAT FISH

The night before the ship's christening, we went to a traditional Door County fish boil. The cook boiled freshly caught Lake Michigan whitefish to perfection in a giant black kettle over a blazing outdoor fire. He finished off the fish boil by throwing some kerosene on the fire, creating a large ball of fire, and making the kettle boil over. The cool air, large fire, fresh fish, and cold beer made for an enjoyable evening.

The next day, the ship's christening was quite memorable, with the minesweeper sliding sideways off a huge wooden platform on the pier and rocking back and forth violently a few times before stabilizing in Lake Michigan's waters. The Admiral's children rode inside the ship's bridge as it was tossed about in the water, which knocked them off their feet and resulted in some minor injuries.

I was glad I had stayed ashore with the Admiral and Janie.

I had planned all the details of that trip for the family. Everything went off without a hitch, and it did seem somewhat like I was part of the family, as there were no problems pulling me into my role as aide.

OFF TO THE INTERNATIONAL TATTOO

On another family trip, we went from Brunswick, Maine, to Halifax, Canada. The Admiral and his wife were going to be guests at the Royal Nova Scotia International Tattoo. The Tattoo was a brilliant display of ceremonial military marching, drums, and bagpipes in a giant coliseum. If you love a military parade and the sound of drums and bagpipes, the Tattoo was the place to be.

We took the *Scotia Prince* to Halifax. The *Scotia Prince* was a large ferry with sleeping quarters, restaurants, and a casino. From 1982 to 2004, it steamed from Portland, Maine, to Yarmouth, Nova

Scotia. The 470-foot-long vessel accommodated up to 1,120 passengers in 250 cabins. For years, the *Scotia Prince* was the ferry of choice for a nice trip out of Portland.

I was part of the family on that trip as well. I drove the car, loaded the luggage, ensured we had the ferry tickets, confirmed the rooms were adequate, made the dining reservations, and ate meals on board with them.

Family or not, that was my job. And I made sure it was done right.

After a long day, I was able to retire to a small stateroom. It had a single porthole looking out to the Atlantic Ocean. It was too cold, windy, and rainy to go out onto the deck, but the porthole view of the ocean was good for me.

To this day, if I have a hotel room with a lake or ocean view or one overlooking an airport runway, it's a good room.

International travel was a challenge. There were language barriers and protocol differences, especially when dealing with a foreign military.

On this trip to Halifax, once we got off the ferry, I drove the Admiral and Janie to the nearby military base to check into our confirmed VIP flag officer accommodations.

It was getting dark when we arrived at the Canadian base. We were eager to get to our rooms.

WE WOULD LIKE TO CHECK IN, PLEASE

We traveled in civilian clothes, so there were no visible stars and no loop. We arrived to check in at the front desk of a sleepy military quarters. It looked dated. A disheveled young Canadian sailor, not too impressed with our presence, was behind the reception desk.

I smiled at him, mentioned that we were there for International Tattoo, and provided our names. As we began some small talk at the check-in counter, the Canadian sailor asked me our names again. He repeatedly typed them into the computer.

He finally said, "I'm very sorry, sir, we do not have rooms for you. Do you have your confirmation numbers?"

"Yes, here you go." I gave them to him.

"There must be some mistake. These are not valid numbers," he replied. Like a *Seinfeld* episode, the sailor stated, "Very sorry, sir. No valid confirmation numbers, no rooms, and we are full. You know we do have Tattoo this week."

Now was the time for me to remain calm when failure seemed imminent and especially not to embarrass the Admiral. He was standing inches away from me with Janie.

I was getting excited. Things had the potential to get heated. I looked at the Admiral. "Sir, if you and Janie wouldn't mind taking a seat over there, I will take care of this," I said, pointing to the brown lounge chairs in the worn-down lobby.

I had no intention of making an international scene, but I knew it was time to increase my voice's amplitude.

I also needed to do so with neither the Admiral nor Janie hearing the debate and being a witness to the collateral damage.

As they walked away, Janie said, "Honey, what are we going to do? There's no other place with rooms around here. We have to get a room. I don't know about you, but I'm really tired."

TELL ME YOUR NAME AGAIN, PLEASE

"Tell me your name again?" I said to the sailor, who was in need of a shave and haircut and smelled like a cigarette.

"Petty Officer Simpson," he stated.

"Okay, Petty Officer Simpson, I need to talk to the senior officer on duty right now. I have confirmation numbers, and I need a room fit for an Admiral and his wife. You have not been able to help me, so perhaps the senior officer can."

I continued. "The Admiral and his wife are here for tomorrow's International Tattoo show as special guests of Admiral Peterson."

"I'm sorry, sir. It is simply because we do have the International Tattoo show that we have no rooms," he tried.

"Wrong answer. Please get the senior duty officer on the phone if you cannot give me a room right now!" I was now getting very agitated. I didn't like doing it, but I could be a real jerk if I had to.

He looked upset. He began dialing a number on the registration desk telephone.

Aware of what I was doing, the Admiral stayed in the lounge area, keeping Janie occupied and glancing at his watch.

The desk clerk handed me the phone. I spoke with the base's senior duty officer, explaining the confusion and that there must be a mistake. Finally, the duty officer apologized profusely and asked me to put the young front-desk clerk back on the phone.

As I had expected, the Canadian admiral, the most senior ranking officer at this base, had a private suite available for his guests. The senior duty officer directed the Canadian sailor to check us into the admiral's VIP suite.

There was a tremendous amount of apologizing. At that point, I was very gracious and thankful. Always be gracious when you get a win.

I got the room keys and escorted them to their room. It was a very nice flag suite.

As for my room, it did not have a water view or look out onto a runway. I got a rather spartan room with a small single bed and a gray wool blanket. The radiator clanked a lot and would not turn off.

I didn't care. I cracked the window. I reviewed the schedule for the next day. Exhausted, I crawled into bed and pulled the blanket up around my neck. I fell asleep in seconds.

Before we left, I noted the names of the senior duty officer and the front-desk clerk so I could write them thank-you letters from the Admiral when we returned to Maine.

I always enjoyed writing these letters.

The letter to the front-desk sailor, with a copy sent to the Canadian admiral, went like this:

> *Dear Petty Officer Simpson,*
> *Thank you for the wonderful reception and hospitality you provided us during our recent stay there for the International Tattoo.*
> *My wife, Janie, and I surely enjoyed the beautiful room. It was the perfect touch to such an amazing trip.*
> *Thank you again for a job well done!*
>
> *Kind regards,*
> *The Admiral*

WHAT I LEARNED

On the family trips, I made sure I never embarrassed the Admiral in front of his family. I was there to take care of the details and fix any messes behind the scenes. People were supposed to like him. It was okay if they disliked me.

While at times I had to be very direct with others, I learned that cussing, yelling, or creating a scene was never the best path forward. It's much better to channel any frustration or agitation into positive action.

Leading by yelling is not leadership at all. No one likes a screamer. I have seen many screamers emerge into leadership positions. They are not leaders. If you want to be promoted to a leadership position, don't lose your temper, and don't be a screamer.

Chapter 17

USE THE RIGHT TOOLS FOR THE JOB

The Admiral taught me to use the right tool to get a job done. If you did not have the right tools, he said, there was a good chance you would screw things up or get hurt. So I learned to be patient and get the right tools for the job.

THE ADMIRAL'S FATHER'S CAR IN JERSEY

During my tenure with the Admiral, we became very close. There were days when he really treated me more like a son than an aide.

One day, he mentioned that his father had an old four-door 1980 green Buick Skylark in New Jersey that he was not using. The Admiral asked if I wanted to buy it. I had a new burgundy Nissan 240SX. A second junker car for my first Maine winter was a great idea.

The Admiral was going to drive down and get it. He wanted to offer it to me.

I told him I would buy it, and we decided on a nominal price. The plan was for me to use it during the winter over the salt-and-snow-covered roads while I stored my Nissan 240SX in an old chicken barn that the owner rented out for winter car storage.

We drove down to New Jersey one day and picked up the car. I drove it back to Maine. The car had been parked for some time, so it needed new tires and some routine maintenance.

I drove my Nissan 240X to the chicken barn, where it would remain all winter. The barn still smelled like chickens, even though none had inhabited it in years.

Like my father, the Admiral was an automobile tinkerer. He had an old red convertible that he had worked on. He stored it in his garage most of the year and brought it out on Maine summer days to take Janie for a ride.

The base had an auto hobby shop with several bays that were available by the hour for self-service vehicle maintenance. He told me we could go there one evening and work on the Buick. We were going to replace some hoses that had started to dry rot, change the oil and all the filters, and replace all the fluids.

The standard maintenance was easy. My father had taught me how to change the oil and fluids when I was in high school on my first car—an ugly mustard-colored Datsun B210.

The Admiral and I went to the auto hobby shop one evening. Once there, I was having difficulty trying to remove one of the radiator hoses. I was using a crescent wrench and a pair of needle-nose lock pliers to loosen a clamp. The crescent wrench kept popping off the nut on the bracket that held the hose in place.

I had scraped my knuckles, and they were bleeding. "Dammit. This one won't come loose, Admiral," I said.

He was watching me. He said, "Mark, it's important when you do a job, any job, that you make sure you use the right tools. Otherwise, you might get hurt, waste your time, or break what you are working on. And none of those are good options. Now, get rid of the crescent wrench and the needle-nose pliers. Go get the socket wrench. Also, get the Liquid Wrench and a couple of rags out of the back of my car."

We sprayed the nut with Liquid Wrench. "Okay, now let's wait ten minutes and go get a Coke out of the machine," he said.

After a few sips of his Coke, he said, "Now, wipe off the bracket with the rags and figure out the right size sockets. Cover your knuckles with the rag as you use the socket wrench."

I did as he said. Within about five minutes, I had the nuts loosened and was able to pull off the old hose.

I bought the car for $300 and used it all winter.

It was a great car for the Maine winter. The heater spooled up quickly. I loved that car.

Over a year later, when I left Maine, I drove the car down Interstate 95 to Naval Air Station Jacksonville, where it stayed on base as my Navy Reserve car for fourteen years!

Always sitting there when I arrived late on a Friday night for a reserve weekend was the Admiral's father's green Buick Skylark.

I was in the reserve P-3 squadron in Jax from 1991 to 2005 and used the car every month. I changed the battery once during that time. The Jacksonville base also had an auto hobby shop where I performed routine maintenance on the car, always making sure I used the right tools.

Near the end of its life, the suffocating humidity of Jacksonville took a toll on the car. The beige fabric on the interior ceiling started to swoop down into the car like a low-hanging cloud. I used some upholstery glue spray sold at an auto parts shop just for that purpose. It worked for a few months but could not beat the Jax heat.

There were times when I got to Jacksonville very late on a Friday night for my reserve weekend. I would drive to the hotel with my left hand on the steering wheel and my right hand holding the fabric up over my head so I could see. I eventually just cut it out with a utility knife, leaving an orange sponge-like material exposed on the car's interior ceiling.

When I stopped going to Jacksonville in 2005, I drove the Admiral's father's car to a junkyard. They said the car had no value, but they would take it off my hands. So I pulled off the license plate and left it there. It had served its purpose very well.

WHAT I LEARNED

Impatience and not using the right tools lead to delays, setbacks, failures, and even injuries. The practical application of this rule is valid not only for car maintenance, but also for tasks in the yard, the kitchen, and handyman jobs around your home. I have also found it quite applicable on the manufacturing factory floor, where safety procedures require the use of specific gear and the right tools to ensure employees' safety.

Be patient. Get the right tools for the job.

Chapter 18

SAY THANK YOU—JANIE'S FUR COAT

Saying thank you goes a long way. I learned that more than thirty years ago from the Admiral.

On one trip near the end of my tenure, we were going to join Janie at an out-of-town event. She was traveling separately by commercial air. We were going to travel on a P-3 and meet her at the destination. The occasion was a formal military event. It was winter. Back then, a flag officer's spouse was a public figure in the eyes of the navy and expected to accompany the Admiral at many military events. Her official travel was guided by ethical rules and approved by the legal team.

I hustled to pick up the Admiral at zero dark thirty from his military quarters. Once there, I grabbed his luggage to load into the car's trunk as I had done like clockwork for months.

This time was a little different.

In addition to his hanging bag, Rollaboard, briefcase, and official navy sword, he handed me a fur coat enclosed in a plastic cover.

"This is Janie's fur coat. It's more important than my sword. Don't lose it," he said. "She doesn't want to hand carry it and will not pack it in her checked baggage, so I told her we would take it."

I knew that "we" meant "me."

You gotta be shittin' me, I thought.

I remembered the initial guidance he had given me. He told me some tasks would be well below my pay grade. I also knew how good he and Janie had been to me.

This was my job. Take care of—and don't lose—the bride's fur coat. And that was exactly what I did. I was the guardian of the fur the whole trip.

We returned to Brunswick a few days later. When we landed, it was dark and cold. The wind was blowing snow on the tarmac when we deplaned.

I loaded the car after the squadron duty officer pulled it up to the P-3. After putting our bags in the trunk, I placed Janie's fur in the back seat.

The heat in the car was blowing. It felt great. We drove the five minutes to the Admiral's residence, where I unloaded the trunk and got the fur out of the back seat. It was wrapped in its plastic cover.

I handed the Admiral his sword and Janie's fur coat. I walked with him up the sidewalk, which was bordered with snow. As we got to the front door, the outside porch light came on. Janie opened the door, and the Admiral handed her the fur. "Here you go, honey," he said.

"Won't you come in for a few minutes, Mark?" Janie asked.

"Oh no, ma'am. I appreciate it, but it has been a long week. You and the Admiral are probably ready for some rest."

Truth be told, I was exhausted. I wanted to get to my rented house, get out of my pungent flight suit, and take a hot shower. I didn't have a fireplace or one of those wonderful Maine wood stoves, but in addition to electric heat, I had an indoor kerosene heater that I would set a foot away from my sofa, and then I would crack a nearby window a quarter inch, cover up in blankets, and doze off to sleep.

"Okay, but thank you so much for taking care of my fur. It made my trip so much easier. I knew I could trust you," she said.

Janie went inside.

The Admiral turned to me and put his hand on my shoulder. He said, "Great job, shipmate. I would have been in big trouble if we lost or screwed up her fur. And I mean that. We've worked half days today, so go home and take the rest of the day off. Thank you, Loop."

I cannot think of a day when the Admiral did not pass my desk on his way out of headquarters or when we had completed an eighteen-hour day on the road when he did not say "Thank you, shipmate" or "Good job today, Loop." As rough as any day had been, I felt motivated working for the Admiral.

There were days when I failed to meet his expectations as an aide, and the Admiral said, "Don't let this happen again." However, the daily praise significantly outweighed the occasional corrective action commentary and made me feel good.

WHAT I LEARNED

Over the past thirty years in the Navy Reserve, law firms, and corporations, I have remembered that feeling of gratitude.

Employees appreciate a steady paycheck and excellent benefits. In addition to that, the goodwill and morale generated when your boss says "thank you" or "good job today" goes a long way.

One of the lawyers who reported to me recently told me I was the first boss who always thanked her and seemed genuinely concerned about her success. That also made me feel great.

The key to being a good leader is to surround yourself with exceptionally talented people. Demand loyalty. Delegate the hard work to them. At every opportunity, give them all the credit for success. And say thank you often.

You can never praise someone too much.

Leaders know the value of expressing gratitude and express it often.

Thank you, Admiral!

Chapter 19

ALWAYS TAKE CARE OF YOUR PEOPLE

By the time I'd been working for the Admiral for over a year, I was confident I would make it through my two-year shore duty tour as his aide. I had gotten to know him so well that I could anticipate his every move. I knew what he was thinking. I knew what he would say.

When he reached for his empty pocket, I handed him a red pen. *(Do you happen to have a red pen?)*

When we entered an office building, I led him to the nearest head. *(I never pass up a head at my age.)*

When we were to meet with another admiral, I reminded him of the name of that admiral's spouse. *(By the way, what is his wife's name?)*

When we checked into a hotel room, I made sure they had a bar of soap in his room. *(A real bar of soap sure would be nice. They need to send that wall soap dispenser back to Europe.)*

When it started to snow, I picked him up in the car thirty minutes earlier than scheduled. *(If it's snowing tomorrow morning, why don't you pick me up thirty minutes early?)*

When he looked around the galley after a meal, I handed him a wooden toothpick. *(Sure could use a wooden toothpick about now.)*

No words were spoken. I just knew. We worked together like a well-rehearsed show.

MY NEXT TOUR OF DUTY

By then, the Admiral had already started talking to me about my next job. Most junior officers would start that discussion about a year out. At that time, one of the most career-enhancing jobs for a P-3 naval flight officer was a disassociated sea tour on an aircraft carrier either as the assistant navigator or a "shooter" on the flight deck itself.

Both jobs appealed to me tremendously because of my love for the sea and my inherent instincts as a sailor, even though I was an NFO. I strongly desired to go to sea to prove I could do it.

I loved airplanes, and I loved the ocean, so my job in a P-3 Orion squadron and working for one of the top P-3 admirals had scratched both itches. I was in the navy, but I flew in a land-based plane. I had spent hundreds of hours on missions covering thousands of square miles over the ocean but always returned to land, not a ship.

At the same time, I was intrigued by a career as a lawyer. I had taken the Law School Admissions Test and started researching law schools. I had talked to the staff JAG. He was a mentor and had originally recruited me to be an aide when I had the collateral duty as a legal officer in my first tour of duty in the Jacksonville squadron. He encouraged me to go for it.

QUITTERS GET FIRED

Back then, the navy considered the aide for an admiral a "golden child" and "the best of the best" in a highly competitive field. When aides told their admirals that they did not want to continue in active service, the admiral usually fired the aide.

Many active-duty officers saw it as an embarrassment to the admiral if their aide wanted to get out of the navy. They considered it a poor reflection of the admiral's leadership and retention ability.

That sentiment was unfortunate, but it was navy culture. It made me mad. I would have served my commitment with honor. I had worked my ass off. But since I chose not to continue active service at the end of my commitment, some navy career-minded officers would consider me a quitter.

The navy officer detailer, whose job was to slot me in my next role, was already penciling me in for the assistant navigator job on one of the navy's newest nuclear aircraft carriers.

Getting orders to a new aircraft carrier, as opposed to one that was twenty years old, was considered a great set of orders. It was to be my reward for a successful aide tour.

I was agonizing about what to do. I had about six more months to decide. I decided to avoid the decision and continue doing an excellent job for the Admiral.

HOW ABOUT NORFOLK?

That changed one day. I answered the phone and was told, "Admiral Callahan would like to speak to your boss. Is he available?"

Admiral Callahan was the flag officer detailer at the Pentagon. A three-star who told baby admirals where they were going next.

I went into the Admiral's office and told him that Admiral Callahan's office was on the phone. He looked up. He had his "cheaters" on as he was editing a draft speech I had given him.

"Okay," he said. "Shut the door on your way out, and connect his office ASAP."

"Aye, aye, sir," I said.

I connected the Admiral with Admiral Callahan. This was not a phone conversation that I listened to.

The call lasted five minutes. I knew when the Admiral hung up because the light associated with his line on my desk phone went out. It then lit up again. He was making another call.

About fifteen minutes later, he called me into his office. "Shut the door," he began. "Mark, I just got verbal orders to Norfolk. They want me to be the base commander and want me to be there in about two months. I'm also going to get a second star."

Norfolk, Virginia, is home to the navy's largest base. The head of that base was a two-star admiral.

"I just told Janie," he said, "and I would like you to come with us."

There was an abrupt silence. My heart sank. I felt like I was going to get sick.

"Wow. That's great, Admiral. Congratulations," I said. I was speechless.

"I know it's as much a surprise to you as it was to me, so you can let me know tomorrow morning," he said.

NO SLEEP

I left the office knowing I had to decide that night on my future. I could decide to stay in the navy, go with the Admiral to Norfolk, and then go to sea on an aircraft carrier. Or tell him I wanted to get out of the navy and attend law school.

That night, I called my dad, a retired navy captain.

How could I disappoint and embarrass the Admiral after all we had been through together? Where was my loyalty?

Dad said, "Son, you are a great naval officer and a great aide, but the day you walk out that door and leave the navy, another great officer will step in. They won't miss you. Go to law school if that's what your heart is telling you to do. It will be just fine."

There is nothing like a father's wisdom to set you straight.

I didn't sleep at all that night.

The next morning when the Admiral arrived at headquarters, he double-tapped the corner of my desk as he walked by, smiling. He said, "Good morning, Loop. So, you going with me?"

I looked up and said, "Sir, can I talk to you in your office?"

"Sure," he said.

I walked into his office, shutting the door on the way in.

"Have a seat," he said.

I was nervous. I sat in the same high-backed chair in front of his desk that I had sat in more than a year before when he gave me the initial guidance.

I took a deep breath.

"Admiral, I am very honored that you have asked me to go to Norfolk with you, but I need to be completely honest with you. I want to go to law school."

He looked up at me. "You mean get out of the navy?"

"Yes, sir."

"Are you sure?" he said.

"Yes, sir."

"Can I talk you out of it?"

"No, sir."

"Are you sure about that?"

"Yes, sir."

"Decision made?"

"Yes, sir."

He stared at me.

"Okay, Mark, what can I do to help you?"

MY LAST FITNESS REPORT

I remember that day more than any of our days together.

In the end, he did help me. He wrote several glowing recommendations to various law schools. He shared with his relief that I was staying in Brunswick and that he'd highly recommended that the new admiral keep me as his aide. He told the new incoming admiral that he really needed me to "train" him. Having both a new flag officer and a new aide at the same time could leave a wide knowledge gap.

Several months later, we had the Admiral's change of command. He and Janie left for Norfolk.

I had a new boss to train!

On my last performance evaluation from the Admiral, when he knew I was transitioning to the Navy Reserve, there was no mention of my decision to leave active service and go to law school. Here's what he said:

> LT Fava is an outstanding naval officer. I selected him from a cast of thousands to be my aide.
>
> LT Fava is bright and energetic. He's not afraid of hard work, and he sees each task through to positive conclusion. He can keep about ten balls in the air at one time and not miss any when they come down. . . . He routinely gives excellent advice.
>
> LT Fava relates well to people. A genuinely nice person, he is widely respected for his empathy and patience. He is a natural leader who carries himself well and who is confident in his own ability. He expresses himself clearly and easily.
>
> As my aide, LT Fava has been exposed to many sensitive issues, and to a wide variety of dignitaries both in and out

> of the military. I can state unequivocally that his integrity is above reproach and that his ethics meet the highest standards. He is mature, and he can be trusted to do the right thing for the right reason.
>
> LT Fava has been given authority and responsibility which far exceeds that normally assumed by a person of his rank and experience. . . . He has my strongest possible recommendation for accelerated promotion to LCDR and for selection to VP aviation command. Even at this early point in his career, he shows clear potential for flag. Simply put, he's as good as there is. A superb officer and a true gentleman.

WHAT I LEARNED

The Admiral could have fired me. Instead, he helped me.

That was authentic leadership. That was one more thing I learned from the Admiral.

Always take care of your people. Do all you can to give them a promising future, even if they decide to depart from the pattern. That's what a true leader does.

Thirteen years later, as a commander in the Navy Reserve, I was selected to be the commanding officer of a Jacksonville P-3 squadron. I commanded two other navy units and was promoted to the rank of navy captain by the end of my career. None of this would have happened if the Admiral had given me "bad paper."

In May 2015, I retired after thirty years and ten days of service, six years on active duty and twenty-four years in the reserves.

CONCLUSION

I learned a lot as an admiral's aide. I hope you have enjoyed this journey and can use this insight. I know it will serve you well. In summary, here are the key takeaways:

- Chapter 1: Know what your boss expects of you when you start a job. If you know the expectations and meet them, you will be successful.
- Chapter 2: Once your boss tells you what they expect, you still need to learn more about your boss. With that knowledge, you will excel. Know your boss better than anyone else.
- Chapter 3: Your job is to get things done. Your success depends on completing tasks that are important to your boss. If you get resistance, use your boss's clout, but do so diplomatically and judiciously.

- Chapter 4: Be on time and meet deadlines. Don't be late as a follower or as a leader. Not much more needs to be said about that.
- Chapter 5: Remember that much of what you learn at work is for work only. That includes business information and personal information. Don't be a gossip. Scuttlebutt might be fun, but it is not your friend.
- Chapter 6: To be effective at accomplishing the task at hand, know all the details better than anyone else. Be the subject matter expert.
- Chapter 7: Once you know all the details, always trust but verify them to ensure flawless execution.
- Chapter 8: Stay organized with simple habits. Count and recount. Think ahead to how what you're doing now will affect the next step.
- Chapter 9: Ask for help when you need it if you make a mistake or are in trouble. Ask early. The sooner the better. People will help you.
- Chapter 10: Keep your composure when things are not going well. Don't be the one who always panics under pressure.
- Chapter 11: Be a creative problem solver when things do not go as planned. Don't give up easily.
- Chapter 12: Always, always be a team player. Help others and contribute to their success. Team players become team leaders.
- Chapter 13: Be dependable and reliable. Do what you say you will do when you say you will do it. Reliability matters.
- Chapter 14: Be loyal to your boss and your employer. Always be guided by integrity. Do the right thing.

- Chapter 15: Know your place and who is senior to you. When you act, have an awareness of the people around you and who they are. Do your homework.
- Chapter 16: Don't be a screamer when you are not getting your way. No one likes a screamer. Some in charge are screamers, but they are not true leaders. Leaders are not screamers.
- Chapter 17: Use the right tools for every job at home and in the office. If you do so, you are more likely to succeed.
- Chapter 18: Say thank you often. Express sympathy, empathy, and gratitude to others at every opportunity.
- Chapter 19: Always take care of your people. Do all you can to invest in their future and make them successful. Do this even if they decide to leave you.

I have used what I learned from the Admiral for many years now. If you are trying to succeed at work and get promoted in any profession, these traits and habits will get you there. They have worked for me. I know they will work for you.

It is not all good luck. You have to be conscious and purposeful in your actions. Don't ever give up. Keep learning.

Since those days, I have had many more bosses and have even become a boss myself. And I have always remembered and used the lessons from the Admiral.

ACKNOWLEDGMENTS

Writing a book is not an easy task. Doing so has been a lifelong dream of mine. I typed the original notes for this book a few years after I finished my job as an aide on a first-generation electric typewriter with a small memory disk more than thirty years ago. Those notes remained in a filing cabinet in a closet for many years. The pages are wrinkled and yellow, but they have finally come to life.

There are quite a few people to thank.

I want to first thank my wife, Dee Ann, and our three daughters, Holland, Dulcie, and Brier. I met Dee Ann at the end of my first navy tour in Jacksonville in 1989, just before I went off to serve the Admiral. I then went to law school after that. We were engaged the night before my law school graduation in 1994 and have been blessed with three beautiful daughters.

Dee Ann and our daughters have seen the best and worst of me over the years. They have put up with many days of my being on the road either for the Navy Reserve or the demands of my legal jobs. I thank them all for their love and support. I hope we enjoy many more summer vacations in Nantucket, holidays at the Grove Park Inn in Asheville, and staycations at The Sanctuary on Kiawah Island. Thank you, and I love you!

I started writing this book when the pandemic hit, as I was tired of the boredom and isolation. About the same time, my mother was diagnosed with ALS. Mom used to walk to church every morning in downtown Charleston, saying hi to everyone along the way. Mom met Dad when they were young students in college at Ole Miss. They got married right after college, as Dad also went into the navy. When he retired as a navy captain in 1987, he gave me his ceremonial navy officer's sword. I had just finished flight school. It remains one of my prized possessions, in addition to a *Black's Law Dictionary* my parents gave me in 1990 when I headed off to law school. Mom and Dad provided editorial guidance and always asked me how the book was going.

This book is dedicated to them. Even on Mom's worst days, she never complained and always said thank you. As she began to lose her speech, she would look at me and struggle to say "Good book." She listened to the entire book as I read it word by word, chapter by chapter, out loud to her. The most she could do was smile or cry tears of happiness and give me a thumbs-up. Mom was proud of "the book," and I am proud to be her published son.

I hate what she went through, but I was blessed to have had my dad, brother Eddie, and sister Debbie there to surround her with care and love. We were all with her when she passed away in July 2023.

To my siblings, Eddie and Debbie, that year was not easy for us. Mom surely did not deserve to leave this world as she did, but I know we surrounded her with love, and you were always there for her—Debbie taking care of her every need and coordinating the doctors, caregivers, difficult conversations, and hospice. Eddie was ever present, always making Mom laugh, taking her on rides out to his weekend house on the Toogoodoo River, and going by to help them every single day. Mom is in a better place now, and I'm grateful for that.

Thank you, Cyndi, for helping us as Mom's caregiver and for the countless hours you spent with Mom and Dad. I know you had your own challenges at home, but your presence, persistence, and positivity made all the difference. You went above and beyond what we could have ever expected and made her life better. Thank you for being part of our family.

It was not easy being a reservist and managing that career along with my primary job and my family. I call that the Reserve Triangle—balancing the ongoing demands of the navy, family, and a primary job. However, my career in the navy was full of wonderful experiences and incredible shipmates. I want to thank all the shipmates with whom I served in VP-56 and VP-62. Some of my best friends are those who flew with me in the P-3 Orion out of Jacksonville, Florida. I thank them for their friendship and service.

I served as an executive officer in VP-62 for TD Smyers and Bryan Quigley. We made a great team. Thank you for your partnership as a Broadarrow and your lifelong friendship. Thanks also for being great officers who emerged as great leaders, even after you retired from the Navy Reserve, in your communities and professions.

In addition to the great people in the navy, over my reserve career, I had wonderful civilian employers who supported me in serving my country. No reservist can be successful without the support of their boss and employer.

In particular, I want to thank Judge David Norton, also a navy veteran, and the federal judge who gave me my first job right out of law school. Judge Norton provided wisdom about life beyond the bench and what it meant to be a good lawyer and a good person. For every career transition I have contemplated since I left his chambers, I have called Judge Norton. He has been on the federal bench for over thirty-three years now and still provides mentorship and life coaching to every young lawyer he hires as his clerk.

I probably never would have been so successful in aviation law without the encouragement of my best friend from high school, Dave Pflieger. Dave was a Naval Academy graduate who got a cross-commission into the air force as a B-52 pilot. Years later, I talked him into going to law school, and he later persuaded me to join him at Delta Air Lines. We're friends for life, along with our two other high school buds, Danny Kassis and Robert Dodds.

I also want to thank Greg Riggs, the general counsel at Delta Air Lines who hired me for my first in-house lawyer job. Greg was the epitome of the wise, sage, southern gentleman lawyer. A consummate professional. I was with him in a conference room at the Airport Renaissance Hotel in Atlanta when 9/11 occurred. Greg taught me how to be a corporate lawyer and the importance of knowing the corporation's business.

Years later, I was hired by Boeing's general counsel, Judge Mike Luttig, in 2010 and then also worked for General Counsel Brett Gerry. Both gave me the opportunity to continue my passion for the law and aviation by working in the world's finest law department at the world's greatest aerospace company. Boeing is iconic, and its people are also.

Judge Luttig built a great law department and entrusted me as his first lawyer in Charleston at a new multibillion-dollar Boeing manufacturing site. After Judge Luttig retired, Brett carried on that tradition of legal excellence, stressing the importance of lawyers being present as business partners and in service to the client. Both were tough and demanding as bosses, but they supported me when I got in trouble once, and I will never forget that.

All of these brilliant lawyers, bosses, and leaders supported me as a lawyer and a naval reservist. Like the Admiral, I got to know them very well also. And I learned from them.

I also want to thank Hank Molinengo, also known by all as "Mongo." Hank was my first lawyer-mentor before I went to law school. As a navy JAG officer, he helped me as a nonlawyer legal officer when I was in my first squadron. He persuaded me to go to Maine to be the Admiral's aide and to work on the same staff he was on. Later, he was instrumental in my going to law school. Hank became an admiral himself. This book would never have happened without Hank grabbing me when I was a young lieutenant and saying, "Fava, you need to come work for the Admiral. You would be great at it! Think about it!" Thank you, Hank—Mongo!

Of course, there's the Admiral. I have to thank him for the impact he had on my life. Little did I know the lessons I learned from being his aide would be banging around in my head for more than thirty years—so much so that I finally had to get them out of my head and onto paper by writing this book. Thank you, sir! You and your "number-one shipmate" were instrumental in my formative years as a naval officer and leader. You are a true shipmate who taught me much about life and success.

This book would not be possible without the talented staff at Amplify Publishing Group (APG), led by Naren Aryal. I started this journey with another publisher and was guided by Chas Hoppe and Hussein Al-Beity. Thank you, Chas and Hussein, for your early coaching and guidance.

When that original publisher shut down overnight, I reached out to Naren, and he was incredibly empathetic, credible, and helpful. Naren and Jess Taylor helped me navigate the process and get on board with APG after a disastrous experience with my first publisher.

An author's decision to publish a book is a very personal decision. I wanted partners who were experts and who would produce a professional product and push me to the end with editorial and professional advice on every detail. My editors, Cheryl Torres and Ray Dittmeier, and APG Director of Production Jenna Scafuri, were exceptional. Every good writer knows the value a talented editorial team brings to their writing, and they brought a lot of value to this book. I also want to thank Director of Design Josh Taggert and the rest of the APG team. Simply put, they know what they are doing and do it exceptionally well.

Most importantly, I want to thank you, the reader. Thank you for letting me share my advice, thoughts, and stories with you. It's such a privilege to be able to do so. Thank you for your time. Know that I always welcome your feedback. You can always reach me on my website at markcfava.com and by email at markcfava@gmail.com. If you subscribe to the mailing list on my website, you'll receive my last unpublished chapter about how I saved the career of the Admiral's replacement. You can also follow me on LinkedIn at linkedin.com/in/markcfava. I love telling these stories live as a speaker also. Many of them are even better told in person. Give me a call, and let's discuss speaking at your event.

I want to thank God for the many blessings He has bestowed on me, especially my family, the jobs I've had, the people I've worked with, and the ability to have such a wonderful naval career.

As the Admiral or any good sailor would say, "I wish you all Fair Winds and Following Seas!" Keep learning! Best of luck, shipmates!

ABOUT THE AUTHOR

MARK C. FAVA is a career aviation lawyer and retired naval flight officer. He is a prolific writer and entertaining speaker. Mark retired from the US Navy as a captain having commanded three units, including an aviation squadron. He has been a law firm partner and a corporate executive lawyer. He has written numerous articles, including "What I Learned from the Judge" in the *SC Lawyer* and "Steering Through a Crisis: Lawyers as Leaders" in *The Washington Lawyer*. As a law school adjunct professor, he has also taught aviation law and legal writing.

Mark was the chief operations attorney at Delta Air Lines on 9/11 and spent years in the navy's P-3 Orion chasing Soviet submarines. He has practiced law for more than thirty years and is currently a vice president at the world's largest aerospace company.

He lives in his hometown of Charleston, South Carolina, with his wife and three daughters. When not working, reading, or writing, Mark enjoys life in the low country and appreciates a cold glass of sweet tea in the summer and a good oyster roast in the fall.